Praise for High Performance Team Coaching

High Performance Team Coaching advances the field of coaching by filling the gap for a practical, yet thoroughly evidence-based model to guide team coaching practice. Drawing on the authors' considerable experience and their recent empirical research, this clearly written, well-documented text provides actionable guidelines and practical strategies for working with teams and makes a genuine and important contribution to the field.

- Dr. Elaine Cox
Editor: *International Journal of Evidence Based Coaching and Mentoring*
Director of Postgraduate Coaching and Mentoring Programmes
Business School, Oxford Brookes University

Team coaching is gaining momentum as an extremely useful practice for organizations. Unfortunately, most coaches and consultants who claim to do team coaching are just repackaging their old group facilitation and individual coaching services. Finally, we have a truly insightful guide that makes the most of advances in team effectiveness research! This is a great addition to the field. Best of all, it is a short, easy read for anyone wanting to follow a practical path that can turn talk of high performance into reality.

- Dr. Ric Durrant
CEC (Certified Executive Coach), PCC (Professional Certified Coach)
Leadership Specialist and Executive Coach

High Performance Team Coaching (HPTC) is a fantastic resource and a 'must read' for all Team Leaders and Coaches. The authors demystify the concepts of creating and sustaining high performance teams and how to lead and coach them. Built upon solid research and investigation along with practical and relevant action steps, it is a resource that will help move your team from average or good, to high performance in any context.

- Lillas Marie Hatala and **Richard Hatala**
Co-authors of *Integrative Leadership: Building a Foundation for Personal, Interpersonal, and Organizational Success*

In their book, Peters and Carr provide a valuable foundation of the research around high performance teams. Leaders and coaches will find their framework for coaching high performing teams very useful in supporting their work.

- Jennifer Britton, MES, CPT, PCC
Author of *Effective Group Coaching* and
From One to Many: Best Practices for Team and Group Coaching

As an experienced professional coach, facilitator and organizational consultant, I support successful teams and their leaders to move to a higher level of performance in order to achieve business results. I had the privilege of partnering with Jacqueline Peters on a company-wide High Performance Team initiative using the High Performance Team Coaching System. This system truly supported the various teams and their team members to become increasingly aware of their current state, what they needed to do to become a high performance team in the future, and how they needed to get there. Although each team was unique, the various team members became enthusiastic and highly engaged in the process of becoming a high performance team. One team even gave a formal thank you card to the leadership team for initiating the program – a first for this company!

- Barb Francis, BA, CEC, PCC
President, Stillwater Coaching Ltd.

High Performance Team Coaching

A Comprehensive System
for
Leaders and Coaches

**Dr. Jacqueline Peters
and
Dr. Catherine Carr**

InnerActive
LEADERSHIP ASSOCIATES INC.

Produced by:

FriesenPress
Suite 300 – 852 Fort Street
Victoria, BC, Canada V8W 1H8

www.friesenpress.com

Distributed to the trade by The Ingram Book Company

This book is dedicated to
Dr. J. Richard Hackman (1940 – 2013).
His work was an inspiration for us and greatly
informed our research and thinking about
team effectiveness and team coaching.

Also by

Dr. Jacqueline Peters and Dr. Catherine Carr

50 Tips for Terrific Teams

Proven Strategies for Building High Performance Teams

www.HighPerformanceTeamCoaching.com

Contents

List of Figures and Tables

Figures

Tables

Acknowledgements

We have much gratitude and appreciation for the many people who have supported us, encouraged us, and contributed to our learning and our lives as we did the research and writing for this book. We had great support from our professional mentors and advisors, Dr. Annette Fillery-Travis, Prof. Peter Hawkins, and Dr. David Lane.

We are grateful for the many teams and leaders who have entrusted us to work with them, allowing us to try new ideas and venture into new territory as we have developed our team coaching skills over the past many years. These teams and leaders remain anonymous in the book but we will never forget who they are, and the instrumental contribution they made to our professional journey.

We have so many friends and colleagues who supported us along the way with patience and empathetic ears. We cannot possibly name everyone, and we regret that we cannot, but know that you are all so precious to us. Catherine would particularly like to acknowledge her fabulous friends Rod Glover and Susan Boegman, and her talented coaching peers, Leslie Henkel and her team at the Public Service Agency of British Columbia. Jacqueline provides special acknowledgement to Denise Still, Colleen Lemire, Anne Scott, and Jennifer Buchanan, who continually provided friendship and needed breaks from research and writing.

We are grateful for our editor, Lee Tunstall, and our early readers who provided invaluable feedback on the book. Many thanks go to Denise Still, Ric Durrant, Janet Wannop, Barb Francis, Judy Au, Debbie Oster, Saida Vuk, Amber Peters, and Joe Peters. Your perspective and comments made the book better! Andrea Lifton played a special role as our graphic designer who was patient with our many edits, and changes.

Above all, we are grateful for the people who supported us most throughout our research and writing journey: our families. Catherine thanks her family including her husband Hersh for all of his support, including providing loving encouragement and pots of tea during those late nights. She would also like to thank her children, Savannah and Sierra, for their patient support and few complaints about eating leftovers... again! Finally, she thanks her son, Ambrose, for several rounds of research advice and Savannah for marketing ideas and a marathon weekend of editing. She also sends appreciation to her parents and mother-in-law for unconditional love and encouragement.

Jacqueline is grateful for her daughter, Natasha, who provided support and encouragement from afar and provided some inspiring conversations to deepen the writing journey! Amber was living at home and overheard endless Skype conversations with Catherine, and endured a mother who was consumed with writing! Amber made sure that Jacqueline got some breaks and gourmet dinners along the way, and provided great editorial feedback! And finally, great appreciation goes to her husband, Joe, who provided encouragement, support, and a listening ear while she pursues her many goals. Joe is a never-ending source of patience, love and friendship.

And, as co-researchers and writing partners, we have immense gratitude for each other. We have a partnership and collaboration that has been incredibly meaningful, supportive, and productive, not only as colleagues, but as friends. We have withstood tests of ambiguity, intensity of workload, and ongoing feedback to each other, and we have emerged as friends. We have shared our appreciation for each other in ongoing ways throughout the journey and this is just another time to mark our gratitude – thanks, Partner!

Finally, we express great appreciation for all of the leaders, coaches and researchers who have come before us. These individuals stimulated our thinking about team effectiveness and how to integrate that body of knowledge into the emerging field of team coaching in organizations. We hope that our work contributes to creating more high performance teams everywhere. Ultimately, people spend an enormous amount of time at work and anything that enhances that experience creates a stronger and happier community in general!

To all of the people who have touched our lives in such meaningful ways over the last four years, we could never have done this without you!

Jacqueline and Catherine

Foreword

For some time I was aware that I had become a less than enthusiastic audience for coaches wishing to discuss team coaching. Given that my usual stance on research and practice is one of intense, and barely contained, curiosity this lack of engagement was obviously a cause for some concern.

Serious reflection on the matter identified the root of my frustration to be the lack of clarity in the field about what we mean by team coaching, a paucity of studies on how it is used and little engagement with its efficacy. There were some notable exceptions from writers such as Peter Hawkins but generally I was left with a sense of confusion and distance from the modality – reminiscent of clutching at fog - but with a vague sense of missing out on a phenomenon with the potential to effect significant change for people and teams within organisations. Every time I thought I had sense of it, I came across, or experienced myself, another example of poor practice and wasted time and effort. I wondered if that was also the experience of those seeking team coaching for themselves or their organisations.

It was in this unimposing environment, but one that was perhaps ripe for change, that Jacqueline Peters and Catherine Carr decided to make their enquiry as practitioner researchers. As their academic advisor I witnessed their open but robustly disciplined curiosity about their own, and each others', practice of team coaching and how this allowed them to bring the much needed clarity to the area, both for coaches and for those wishing to experience team coaching. With a combination of systematic field research and an intense scrutiny of the literature they have developed a system of high performance team coaching that is fit-for-purpose and accessible for practitioners but with an appropriate and transparent evidence base. It provides the framework and underpinning that will allow this much-needed modality to achieve its potential.

Dr. Annette Fillery-Travis, BSc, MA, PhD, CChem, FRSC
M/DProf Programme Coordinator, Middlesex University
Member of the Steering Group of the International Centre
for the Study of Coaching

High Performance Team Coaching

A Comprehensive System
for
Leaders and Coaches

Introduction

"Certainly the senior leadership's view of the department has been elevated [as a result of team coaching] and as soon as you see a team as more high performing, you have more faith and trust and you believe that they can accomplish more."

- VP, Corporate Finance Leadership Team, Multinational Corporation

Only one out of five teams is high performing; a rather dismal statistic (Wageman, Nunes, Burruss, and Hackman, 2008). High performing teams continually push for success and are not satisfied with the status quo. Instead, they search for proven approaches and opportunities to continually "push the envelope" to achieve even greater performance, effectiveness, and success. If you are reading this book, you are likely a team leader, manager, team member, or coach who wants to raise the bar for your team. We created the High Performance Team Coaching System so that teams can achieve more together, improve engagement, and get results. This system is a comprehensive approach that we have developed and refined over a decade of working with teams.

The High Performance Team Coaching (HPTC) system is designed for anyone who coaches a team: team leaders coaching their own teams, internal HR professionals who want to better support their client teams, or professional team coaches who want to implement a clear, systemic, and evidence-based approach to team coaching. We developed the HPTC system so that organizations of all sizes can increase the effectiveness of their teams and team projects.

Our own experience as leaders and team coaches is that team management and leadership is complex. If not well prepared, leaders may be forced to rely on anything from gut feelings to guesswork. Without the benefit of research and proven systems, it may be too late when organizations realize they cannot adequately help their teams produce competitive results. How a team creates its deliverables too often seems mysterious, opaque, and fraught with interpersonal conflict, none of which contribute to a high level of confidence for the leader or the team members. Sometimes leaders are not aware of the internal dynamics of the team because they are not directly involved with team members on a day-to-day basis, or they're not sure how to effectively manage their team.

The result is that all too often leaders apply what they have intuitively learned about leading teams, not necessarily what research has shown to be most effective. Although common sense often works, there can be faster and easier ways to achieve team goals if you know what activities produce the most benefits. To speed up your learning curve, we reviewed years of team effectiveness research to uncover exactly what actions, structures, and processes drive team success.

Teams can also benefit and accelerate their collective performance by assigning an internal, or hiring an external, impartial team coach. This person's sole objective is to help the team, both individually and collectively, find ways to work well together that will help meet or exceed the team's goals. An external coach or human resources consultant may be particularly helpful when a leader is balancing the many demands of forming a new team, is new to coaching, or has a central role in the team dynamic that needs to change.

Team coaching in sports has been around for ages; the idea itself is not new. As well, team leaders have been coaching their teams to varying degrees as long as there have been leaders of teams. However, team coaching as a separate, defined discipline within organizations is a relatively new field and as such, the term is not well defined or applied in the coaching and organizational development world. It has been used as an umbrella term that includes team facilitation and team building, among other team interventions. This range of interventions is the reason we often get asked, "What exactly should a team coach do?" This is the question we aim to address in this book.

When we speak with coaches, the most frequent approach to team coaching we hear is "in-the-moment" team coaching during meetings or facilitation of team offsite events. During these meetings, coaches often focus on helping the team ask better questions, intervening when they see a team conversation going off-course, encouraging equal participation, and fostering safety and trust for team members in team meetings. All of these actions are important; however key elements of effective team coaching are missing.

If team leaders and coaches are committed to enhancing team performance, there is more to do than "in-the-moment" coaching. Team leaders inherently sense this, but they don't always know how to expand beyond this. New team coaches may also be confused about what else to do when working with a team and consequently may over rely on basic non-directive coaching conversation competencies they learned when training to do individual coaching.

Whether the team coach is the leader or a professional coach, the basic skills of coaching are essential. However, the broader goal of supporting overall team effectiveness places significantly greater demands upon the leader or coach. Additional skills in team assessment, facilitation, change management, and consultation are also required to be effective as a High Performance Team Coach. Further training may be necessary to support a team coach to acquire these skills.

Thus, we propose that the most effective team coaching includes "in-the-moment" coaching, team leader coaching, and additional assessment, design and review steps that have been shown to be essential for team success and proven to boost team performance. It is, therefore, vital to understand these key steps and performance boosters, and to weave them into the natural business cycle of the team.

Given this broader focus and context for team coaching, we developed the following definition for the High Performance Team Coaching system:

> High Performance Team Coaching
> is a comprehensive and systemic approach
> designed to support a team to maximize
> its collective talents and resources to
> accomplish and exceed the goals
> required by the organization.
> (Carr and Peters, 2012:258)

If we break this definition down, the HPTC system is **comprehensive**, meaning that it is an approach that supports team effectiveness through the key stages of team development, from the beginning to the end of a team's business cycle. The system is not just about coaching the team in meetings or focusing solely on interpersonal dynamics. It is an approach that addresses the many factors that drive team effectiveness in a wide variety of circumstances., such as supporting a change process over time, or launching a new brand or business agenda

The HPTC system takes a **systemic approach**, meaning that it is not just focused on supporting the internal dynamics of the team, but it also concentrates on the organizational system in which the team operates. This systemic focus is a growing emphasis of experienced practitioners and team coaching thought leaders, like Peter Hawkins, who wrote the book, *Leadership Team Coaching.* An example of this would be interviewing stakeholders as well as team members on the strengths, challenges and opportunities of a team.

The HPTC system is deliberately **designed to support a team** by providing ongoing coaching from team beginnings to endings. It outlines clear steps and strategies that can be implemented by the team leader or an internal or external coach in a step-by-step manner. As it is divided into six modules, it is also flexible enough to customize to the needs of the team throughout the many beginnings and endings that naturally occur within team projects and business cycles.

Although the system lends itself to a sophisticated and systemic team coaching approach, there is also built-in flexibility to be able to assess a team's needs and apply only some phases of the system as required. Sometimes the realities of organizational life are that a team will only commit to certain phases, or will start by committing to a few at first and then will add more phases down the road. Additionally, many teams today are thrown together quickly and disbanded within cross-team configurations and rapid project cycles (Edmondson, 2012). The HPTC system is flexible enough to support all kinds of teams with its phased approach to team coaching, although implementing all six phases of the HPTC system is ideal to maximize team effectiveness.

The next part of the HPTC definition is to **maximize the team's collective talents and resources**. Ultimately, the best teams ensure that all team members fully participate and engage in achieving its goals. Ideally, everyone's talents and efforts are leveraged so that the team reaps the benefits of the diversity and uniqueness of each individual on the team. The HPTC system is focused on creating conditions and providing ongoing coaching that support individual and collective success.

The last component of the HPTC definition is to **accomplish and exceed the goals required by the organization**. Ultimately, teams exist to achieve results. The HPTC system is focused on the outcomes that the team must produce for the organization to be successful. It is about ensuring that goals and measures are defined and then providing support, guidance and coaching to achieve the goals. The highest performing teams aim not only to meet goals; they strive to exceed those expectations. An excellent team coach, whether it is the leader or someone else, keeps the team's highest aspirations and desired outcomes in mind. They help the team consider **what** the present and the future requires of the team to achieve and **how** the team can best do this.

Overall, the HPTC system is a robust, flexible coaching approach that is grounded in both real-world experience and best practice research about what makes teams effective. Throughout the book, we have noted the major researchers whose work provides the evidence base for this team coaching system. These references will help leaders and coaches see how the components of the HPTC system align with knowledge about what has been shown to drive team performance.

We have spent many years working in organizations and have seen first-hand that most leaders are too busy to find the time to read and incorporate research on teams and leadership on their own – they have teams to lead and organizations to run! This book synthesizes the literature and research for team leaders, managers, and coaches. There is also a full list of references at the back of the book that we used in the research. This book is for you if you want to be current and performance focused without having to read hundreds of books and articles.

Summary

The comprehensive High Performance Team Coaching system is a unique, one-stop approach for effectively coaching a team throughout its business cycle. It has a systemic approach that is focused on performance and results both within the team and with the stakeholders beyond the team. The HPTC system provides a strong, evidence-based team coaching approach for leaders and coaching practitioners alike. The system has been published in the *International Coaching Psychology Review* (Carr and Peters, 2013) and has been tested over ten years with many teams who reported successful outcomes.

How to use this Book

This book is organized to provide leaders and coaches with the research background and rationale behind the High Performance Team Coaching system in the first three chapters. Chapter one provides a summary of the characteristics and measures of a high performing team. Chapter two covers five different team interventions and the philosophy of team coaching that underlies the HPTC system. Finally, chapter three highlights the three stages that occur naturally in a team, and how to maximize performance in each stage. The HPTC system diagram in Figure 1 is a visual that will help orient you as you read the background to the HPTC system that follows in the first three chapters.

If you are not as interested in all of the background and research behind the model, you can skip directly to chapter four, which presents the High Performance Team Coaching system on a single page and guides you through the components in detail. You will see how each component is deliberately sequenced and linked to team effectiveness research, as well as the natural life cycle of a team. Chapter five provides a few ideas for each of the six phases of team coaching that will allow leaders and coaches to get started implementing the HPTC system. Chapter six is a bonus chapter including five tips for transforming teams chosen from one of our other books, *50 Tips for Terrific Teams* (Peters and Carr, 2013). You can apply these tips immediately on their own or as part of your approach to coaching your team.

At the beginning of each chapter, we highlight a quote from the teams who participated in our in-depth, team coaching case study research, although we have successfully used this system with other teams as well. Finally, we include a detailed reference list for readers who have an interest in reading more about the research that informed this team coaching system and approach.

Figure 1:   Overview of the High Performance Team Coaching System
© Peters and Carr, 2013

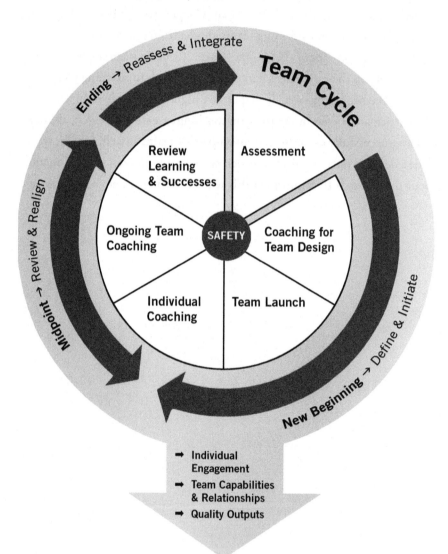

Team Effectiveness

CHAPTER 1

Defining the High Performance Team

"We were a top team work unit before we did team coaching and we got in the game so that is the good news. What happens when you are on top though is to keep thinking of pushing that envelope because it becomes the baseline - you can never rest on your laurels – and we never do. We continue to push ourselves."

- Senior leader of a top performing Employee Engagement leadership team

What is a high performance team? Let's start by defining a team. Katzenbach and Smith's classic 1993 book, *The Wisdom of Teams*, defines a team as:

> A team is a small number of people with complementary skills who are committed to a common purpose, performance goals, and approach for which they hold themselves mutually accountable.
> (Katzenbach and Smith, 1993:45)

This commitment to a mutual, interdependent purpose is one of the most important distinctions between groups and teams. We note other common differences between working groups and teams in Table 1.

Table 1:   Differences between Groups and Teams

GROUP	TEAM
Collection of people who: • report to the same person • work within the same kind of function or department • require little interdependence to achieve objectives • have minimal mutual accountability • are not rewarded for achieving common goals	A relatively small number of people (3 to 12) who: • share common goals and the responsibility for achieving them • share rewards for achieving the goals

←――――――――――――――――――――――→

1   2   3   4   5   6   7   8   9   10
GROUP   **TEAM**

As with most things in life, the difference between a team and a group is not black and white. Teams will fall somewhere on a continuum of operating in more team-like ways to behaving in more group-like ways. We suggest that teams rate themselves on the group-team continuum in Figure 1 as a way to gauge their current functioning as being more group-like or more team-like. Next, teams can discuss and determine how the team needs to function in order to achieve their goals.

Most groups act in some ways like a group, and in other ways like a team, often scoring between two to nine on the group-team continuum rather than being fully situated at one end or the other. It is important not to try to force a group to be a team if the members really do not have any common goals, accountability, or rewards. This creates unnecessary work and expectations. Often work groups are labelled as teams, but they act like independent people who happen to be in the same function, group, location, etc. We view high performance teams as groups of people who work together in interdependent ways and score themselves closer to the team definition than the group definition. Components of the HPTC system may be helpful for groups, but it is designed for teams that must work together at least some of the time to achieve their goals.

To determine what interdependent goals a team might have, ask this simple question:

> **What must we do together**
> **to meet our goals?**

Given this context, "What is a high performance team?" We suggest that:

> **A high performance team is one**
> **that meets or exceeds the goals set**
> **by the organization and/or those it**
> **has set for itself.**

In sports, a high performance team is easily recognizable as one that wins the World Cup or the Super Bowl. In science, it refers to a team that makes a breakthrough discovery such as identifying a cure for a disease. In business, a high performance team is one that meets its objectives by developing a new product, finding a new way to cut costs, or successfully leading the organization to meet the goals of its stakeholders. Ultimately, a high performance team is one that allows the business to meet and exceed its overall objectives. In short, the team's performance is greater than the sum of its parts.

High performance teams come in all shapes and sizes. The team that launched the Curiosity Rover to Mars included a huge team of scientists and technicians who worked in close cooperation over many years towards a common goal. There may be a team of a half-dozen staff across an organization that is responsible for the rollout of a key new product or key deliverable. In addition, a team may be just you and your two colleagues, but even a team of two or three can have difficulty working in harmony and achieving their results!

Hindsight is 20-20, but to see clearly in the moment can be challenging. While it is no problem to identify teams that are successful once they've reached their goal, it is much more difficult to assess a team's likelihood for success when the project is just beginning or is in process. So, how can you know when your team is on the right track and will produce positive results? It's a serious question because the stakes can be very high.

For a company that is developing a new product, the failure of the Research and Development team can have devastating consequences. When a team is charged with finding a new manufacturing partner, if they don't make the right choice, the results can be poor quality products and angry customers, or worse, financial and reputational losses. And perhaps most commonly, if a team chooses to move a project along as fast as possible with little attention to quality or the consequences of shortcuts, the results can be missed opportunities, failure to meet the stakeholders' needs, and poor performance. For leadership teams who have less well-defined deliverables, a lack of cohesiveness and clarity of direction can create an organization that is political, scattered, and underperforms to the board's, investors', and/or customers' expectations.

Sometimes a team starts to flounder and its members quickly seek guidance to get back on track. It is worse when teams plod along, and when you inquire about their progress they say, "Everything is fine." No one ever knows the depth of the team's mediocrity until poor processes, systems and structures are entrenched and it is too late to make an easy recovery.

To lessen mediocrity and create a more successful, transparent trajectory, there are three things every team needs to openly and clearly articulate. Teams need to be clear about where they are going, how they will get there, and how to know when they have arrived. This may sound like common sense but in reality, all too many teams skip or short circuit one or more of these steps, to their detriment. Broadly, these three steps are to:

1. **Assess.** Leaders and the coaches who work with them need to find out what the team's stakeholders expect from the team. Stakeholders of the team and team coaching include not only the participating team members but may also include the board, executive team, customers, suppliers, and internal clients.

2. **Chart the Course.** Put the plan in place to meet the goals, expectations and timelines required of the team. Clarify expectations about how the team will work together to achieve the results the team is collectively seeking.

3. **Measure Progress and Results.** As time progresses, teams need a way to know if they are achieving results. If the team is not meeting stakeholder expectations for the required results, they need to be able to figure out why and how to fix it. Clear success measures or the use of a balanced scorecard can be helpful to track progress and results for both the team members themselves and other teams and stakeholders who rely upon the team's work.

The HPTC system incorporates these three steps of assessment, charting the course, and measuring progress and results. Top-performing teams implement these steps as a matter of course, and they are especially valuable for new or underperforming teams. Every team's performance can be improved, and in addition to intervening in a struggling team, savvy managers will also use these strategies to improve and ensure that the performance of highly competent teams stays on course. This focus on always improving the team's performance may be what separates a really good team from a truly great team.

As we venture into the research and principles behind the High Performance Team Coaching System, Table 2 provides an overview of the key points and definitions that we incorporate and discuss in this chapter.

Table 2:   Overview of Key Definitions and High Performance Team Coaching Research

Definition of a Team	"A **team** is a small number of people with complementary skills who are committed to a common purpose, performance goals, and approach for which they hold themselves mutually accountable." (Katzenbach and Smith, 1993:45)
Definition of High Performance Team Coaching	"**High Performance Team Coaching** is a comprehensive and systemic approach designed to support a team to maximize their collective talents and resources to accomplish and exceed the goals required by the organization." (Carr and Peters, 2012:258)

Three Essential Steps for Team Success	1. Assess. 2. Chart the Course. 3. Measure Progress and Results.
Three Key Drivers of Team Performance	1. Team design and structure (60% of performance). 2. Team launch (30% of performance). 3. Ongoing Team coaching (10% of performance).
Three Times in a Team Cycle when Coaching has the Greatest Impact	1. **Beginnings:** This includes the actual initiation of a new team OR a new beginning for an established team through a new team project, strategy, major initiative, fiscal year, or business cycle. 2. **Midpoints:** The approximate midpoint in the team's work together as a project team or a functional or leadership team that is implementing a new strategy, initiative, fiscal year, or business cycle. 3. **Endings:** The dissolution of the team or the completion of the team's work on a project, strategy, initiative, fiscal year, or business cycle.
Three Outcomes / Measures of a High Performance Team	1. Quality outputs. 2. Team capabilities and relationships. 3. Individual engagement.

The Three Key Drivers of a High Performance Team

What are the elements that differentiate a high performance team from an ordinary team? Is it luck? The people? A great boss? Having the freedom to experiment? Serving coffee and doughnuts at meetings?

Broadly, there are three key elements that have been found to contribute significantly to team performance and success. They are:

1. Team design and structure.
2. Team launch.
3. Team coaching.

What is the relative importance of these three areas? Richard Hackman (2011) has studied team effectiveness for over 40 years and suggests that:

- 60 per cent of team performance can be attributed to team structure and design.
- 30 per cent to an effective team launch.
- 10 per cent to competent team coaching.

These percentages are likely not exact, especially not in all circumstances. However, research indicates that these percentages are generally accurate, and as a result, they inform the framework of the HPTC system. Further, these three areas can and often do overlap in timing and implementation. As a result, team coaches using this High Performance Team Coaching system can directly influence the team coaching component and the team launch component through the coaching approach and activities they provide.

External team coaches are also advised to start by coaching, and sometimes even educating, the team leader, since many leaders are not aware of how to best structure and design their team to maximize performance. Clearly, team leader education is important to include given that proper team structure and design represents up to 60 per cent of team performance.

The Three Outcomes / Measures of a High Performance Team

Ultimately, the expected outcome from any team coaching process should be enhanced team effectiveness. There are three key areas to assess or measure team effectiveness, which we have adapted from the measures outlined by Wageman, Hackman and Lehman (2005) in their work on team performance:

1. Quality outputs.
2. Team capabilities and relationships.
3. Individual engagement.

The first measure of team effectiveness is the quality of the outputs the team achieves. Whether the output is a product, service, or leadership, this is the ultimate reason the team is together, so it is the most important measure of effectiveness. This is "what" the team needs to achieve. It includes outputs and outcomes like a new product, a sales goal, or a completed merger. For senior leadership teams, it is the effective stewardship of the people in the organization to meet stakeholder expectations and targets. This can include customer loyalty and employee engagement. The important guiding question is: "How well is the team achieving what it is meant to do?"

The second measure of team effectiveness is the team's capabilities and relationships, which is their individual and collective ability to work effectively to achieve their goals. This is broadly "how" the team goes about achieving what they need to achieve. Does the team improve at delivering on their goals as they work together over time? Do their relationships become more productive? Are they agile in times of increasing flux and change (Parsons and Carr, 2013)?

The third measure of team effectiveness is the level of individual engagement, positive feelings and connection to the team that each member demonstrates, as individual commitment by all members is required for success. Can members say that the team they work in is one they are excited to be a part of and one that supports their individual aspirations and growth?

Summary

This brief overview of the elements and outcomes of high performance teams highlights that effective team interventions, like team coaching, need to be consciously and deliberately created. This means ensuring that there is time taken to assess, chart the course, and make a plan for measuring the required results. Once this foundation is created, leaders need to ensure that teams are structured and designed well. They also need to launch the team properly and then coach the team to ensure team members maintain their focus and sustain momentum on the course they have charted together, while staying adaptive and flexible to changing priorities.

Finally, overall team effectiveness is measured in three key ways. First is the achievement and production of quality outputs. Second is the development and quality of the team capabilities and relationships. Third is the level of individual team member engagement and commitment to the team. The HPTC system supports teams to achieve all of these measures of effectiveness.

CHAPTER 2

Team Coaching

"But ultimately when you get to the end and you get a finished product that is so far superior to anything that has come out previously, it's worth butting heads and I think people can see the result. I think team coaching has absolutely been part of that process."

- Team member, Senior Leadership Team in Government

Team coaching in organizations is a relatively new field and as such, little research has been completed to date. Most of the work published is comprised of short case descriptions about what leaders and/or team coaches have done, or processes they have followed in their team interventions (Carr and Peters, 2012). Until recently, most organizational coaching seems to have been primarily centred on coaching the individual, not the team. Although organizational development specialists have done variations of team coaching over the years, it appears that team coaching as its own discipline and professional service is relatively new, appearing over the last 10 to 15 years.

Many European coaches have published about team coaching, including Devillard (2000) who wrote about team dynamics and developed Team-Scan, a team assessment tool. Cardon (2003) wrote about systemic team coaching. Moral (Giffard and Moral, 2007; Moral, 2009) discussed systemic and developmental team coaching and assessment, and Hawkins (2011) wrote a robust leadership team coaching guide for practitioners.

Hackman and Wageman, prominent North American researchers and authors of many books and articles in the team effectiveness field, described team coaching in 2005 as "Direct interaction with a team intended to help members make coordinated and task-appropriate use of their collective resources in accomplishing the team's work." This means that team coaching can include a number of different interventions and approaches, as discussed in the next section.

The Five Levels of Team Interventions

Every team is unique. No two teams require exactly the same level of intervention or coaching. Some require a top-to-bottom overhaul, while others may require only a minor course correction to achieve the best possible results. The degree of intervention lies on a continuum from minimal to comprehensive (Hawkins, 2011), as illustrated in Figure 2. The five levels of team coaching are meant to be adapted and customized to each specific situation, with the more comprehensive levels requiring greater skill and knowledge from the team coach.

Hawkins' continuum compares five team interventions, and demonstrates the flow from traditional forms of intervention to more current, complex and multidimensional systems of team coaching. Team leaders and coaches advance along the continuum and support their teams to consider their deeper purpose, the needs of their internal and external stakeholders, and the team's wider impact on their organization and the global community as a whole. The urgent problems facing organizations today reinforce the need for more effective team coaching that can focus more on the multi-layered, more complex team coaching interventions at the right side of the continuum, which are the primary focus of the HPTC system.

The simplest intervention or form of team coaching on the continuum is **team facilitation**. Facilitation is purely a short-term process approach to support a team to hold an effective meeting or event. Facilitation is a legitimate team intervention and may be an element of team coaching, but its focus on process instead of content is insufficient for helping a team to accomplish its work over time and in the everyday workplace.

Figure 2: Continuum of Team Coaching and Team Interventions

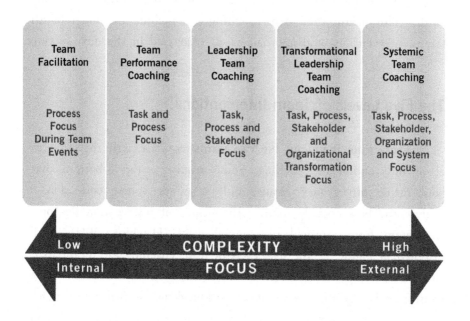

Source: Adapted from Hawkins, 2011:62

The next intervention is **team performance coaching**, which has an additional focus on supporting the achievement of tasks, not just the process of making a meeting flow better. Coaches working at this level ask questions about goals and intervene to support the team to stay focused and working productively towards their purpose and goals.

Moving further to the right on the continuum, **leadership team coaching** is a coaching approach that is focused specifically on leadership teams. When coaching leadership teams, coaches attend to the process and tasks of the team, while adding a focus on how team members lead their direct reports and their department or organizations. There is also attention placed on how members influence stakeholders.

A variation of leadership team coaching is the fourth intervention, the more complex approach of **transformational leadership**

coaching. This level of coaching includes all previously mentioned tasks and adds a focus on transforming the business beyond the current performance of the team. How do you achieve this? By supporting the team to interact and work together over the period required to achieve the transformation goal, which is often six months to a year or more.

If external, the team coach would periodically participate in team meetings and may even do individual coaching to support the team. The purpose here is to get team members to effectively work together within and between meetings to achieve the organization's transformational goals.

Finally, the fifth level, **systemic team coaching** is a complex and comprehensive process by which the leader or a designated team coach works with an entire team, both as a group and individually, in order to help them improve both their collective performance and how they work together. Systemic team coaching also helps teams develop their collective leadership to more effectively engage with all their key stakeholder groups to jointly transform the wider business. Hawkins makes the valid point that leaders and coaches who aim to assist teams making this kind of transformational change need a high degree of coaching skill at this level.

The HPTC system is ideally suited to coaching leadership teams that are working to make systemic or transformational change throughout the organization and beyond. However, even project teams, long-term teams, or functional teams such as Human Resources or Finance can use the HPTC system because the specific content or focus of the team is not important. All teams go through similar cycles and stages, from starting to completing their work together. The six phases of the HPTC system are structured to match a team's natural beginning, midpoint, or end stage, so the system can be used for almost any team at any point of development. Every team requires many of the same conditions, structures, and processes implemented to be successful.

The HPTC system focuses on coaching the whole team together, with a strong suggestion to coach other team members individually when needed. Individual coaching is particularly important for the team leader if the coaching is being delivered by a person external to the team. Individual team leader coaching and whole team coaching support the team to develop structures and agreements that enhance productivity in team meetings and in their ongoing work between meetings and coaching sessions.

Further, the HPTC system incorporates processes, structures and frameworks to engage both the team and stakeholders in conversations about what the team needs to do to have a wider impact within their organizational context. Systemic team coaching would typically require all elements of the HPTC coaching system to be applied, but almost every team can benefit by carrying out most, if not all of the HPTC phases.

Internal and External Focus

Of the five team coaching interventions described in the previous section and illustrated in Figure 2, the first two, facilitation and team performance coaching, are defined by their internal focus. This comprises the internal processes and dynamics of what a team is working on and how they learn to work together. A broader and more powerful approach to team coaching balances this internal focus on the team's functioning with a focus on the external stakeholder relationships and performance expectations. This external focus means supporting teams to reach beyond simply how they are working together and move towards how they are impacting others and what other stakeholders need from them to be successful.

Wageman and her colleagues wrote a book called *Senior Leadership Teams: What it Takes to Make them Great* (2008) and indicated that leaders who have as much of an external focus as they do an internal focus lead the highest performing senior leadership teams. This external focus is most prominent in the three coaching approaches on the right hand side of the continuum: leadership team coaching, transformational coaching, and systemic coaching.

A Safe Environment

> Trust is an outcome
> of having ongoing experiences
> of feeling safe with others.

Just as most workplaces have a "safety first" mantra for physical safety, this mantra is equally important for psychological and/or emotional safety. In fact, psychological safety is the factor that underpins the entire HPTC system, as it is one of the defining features of all coaching. In our case studies, safety to participate, be honest, and disclose were central to what the participants saw as key turning points that impacted their team performance (Carr and Peters, 2012). Other researchers have also emphasized the importance of psychological safety and the connection between a safe environment and enhanced team performance (Buljac-Samardžić, 2012, Edmondson, 1999).

"Safety" is not the same as "trust", but safety is a critical component for building trust. Trust is often harder to describe and define behaviourally, as we discovered while reading the many different definitions and categories of trust listed in the academic literature. We believe that trust is actually an outcome of having ongoing experiences of feeling safe with others. Trust is more of a psychological label that is applied when people feel safe in a conversation, interaction, or relationship. Psychological safety is an in-the-moment experience that can be physiologically measured by tracking changes in a person's heart rate, and blood pressure (Gottman, 2012). Trust is a term that people typically apply to relationships when they have felt safe over a period of time.

We have found in our research that the coach's manner and actions both model and set the stage for team safety. A growing body of research in coaching and an extensive body of research in counselling confirm the link between a positive working alliance with the coach / counsellor and positive client outcomes (Horvath and Symonds, 1991; Marshall, 2006). But it is not enough for the team coach to create safety for the team. Every member of the team needs to behave in ways that contribute to a safe environment.

This means that if the team leader is not the team coach, there is a particularly strong need for the leader to reinforce and demonstrate safety and trust-building behaviours. The goal is to feel safe enough to disclose, challenge, fail, learn, and succeed together. To achieve this, all team members must be accountable to the agreements and behaviours that support themselves and each other to feel safe. Safety is at the centre of the HPTC system in order to reflect its importance. Ultimately, without psychological safety, honest disclosure, and debate, performance will be less than ideal.

Summary

The HPTC system is a way to formalize, define, and systematize a robust team coaching approach that allows leaders, HR professionals, and internal and external coaches to focus on proven strategies that increase team effectiveness and performance. Taking a systemic approach like this can be especially productive for leadership and high-level teams who are guiding transformational change in their organizations.

At the same time, almost every team will benefit from focusing externally as much as internally. Teams simply can't be as effective when they work in a vacuum of their own shared beliefs and goals. All teams have outside factors that affect them and other stakeholders who have a vested interest in their results. Keeping an eye on things external to the team is an important reminder for the team leader and team coach. It is all too easy to get caught up in the internal dynamics of a team.

Finally, all team interventions require a safe environment to be optimally effective, especially team coaching. It is important to remember that "safety first" is not just about wearing steel toed boots and hard hats!

CHAPTER 3

Three Stages in a Team's Life Cycle

*"I do think that this type of coaching is really import-
ant if you are going to roll out changes within a group or a
new direction. And that new direction goes hand in hand
with coaching, and gets people working together and making
changes. [Team coaching] makes [change] more focused and strategic."*

- VP, Corporate Finance, Multinational Corporation

One of the most popular ways of thinking about team cycles is the popular forming, storming, norming, and performing stages of team development that Bruce Tuckman defined in the 1960s. This is a good model to consider when thinking about teams, although some teams can get
stuck in certain stages or may cycle back and forth between these stages.

Another simple model from University of California researcher,
Connie Gersick (1988), is based on a concept called punctuated equilibrium. This concept focuses on the three natural stages that occur during a
team's work together from a timeline or milestone perspective: the beginning, midpoint, and ending stages. Forming, storming, norming, and performing definitely occur within these three natural stages; however, Gersick's model is a simpler and more predictable framework for guiding team
coaching efforts and focusing the team on the tasks required at each stage.

The High Performance Team Coaching system draws on Gersick's
research by recognizing the beginning, midpoint, and ending stages of a
team's natural cycle. Further, the system suggests coach or leader interventions
and strategies that appropriately match each team phase. Gersick identified

that teams are only able to make significant change at these three times in their life cycle, and that changes at other times are incremental at best, hence the term "punctuated equilibrium." Being aware of these critical change periods is important when determining the best timing and focus for coaching interventions.

Figure 3: Three Times in a Team Cycle when Coaching has the Greatest Impact

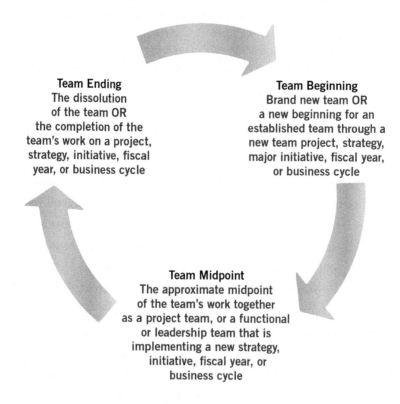

Team Ending
The dissolution
of the team OR
the completion of the
team's work on a project,
strategy, initiative, fiscal
year, or business cycle

Team Beginning
Brand new team OR
a new beginning for an
established team through a
new team project, strategy,
major initiative, fiscal year,
or business cycle

Team Midpoint
The approximate midpoint
of the team's work together
as a project team, or a functional
or leadership team that is
implementing a new strategy,
initiative, fiscal year, or
business cycle

Source: Inspired by Gersick, 1988

Gersick's model is deceptively simple but highly important as change can be stimulated at key points of the team's life cycle. Gersick states that a team hits the ground running early in their work together. Norms and strategies are usually implicit at this beginning point, and the team usually doesn't make many changes in the way they work together until the approximate midpoint of their task, project, goal, or fiscal year. It is at this natural midpoint of the team's work that team members typically consult with others and often fundamentally shift how they are working together as a team. They become aware that they are moving into the second half of their project or defined work timeline and they think about their project in new and transformative ways at this midpoint.

Finally, the team also gathers speed near the end of their project or business cycle. This stage is often neglected by teams and coaches, with very little closure or reflection offered at the end of a team cycle to identify and benefit from lessons learned.

Any coaching interventions that focus on strategy or shifting how a team works together will not have much impact between the beginning stage when the team initially begins their work, and when the team hits their reflective midpoint stage. For example, as any team player knows, the very early brainstorming phase of a project is not a good time to demand finalized plans; and conversely, the delivery date is no time to encourage "out of the box" thinking.

Team development needs to match the team's natural rhythm and performance requirements at the various stages of the team's business or life cycle. Team coaching needs to be flexible enough to help the team respond to their unique challenges and changes during the journey of working together, yet also keep the end goal and desired results in mind. The next section describes each of these three stages, beginning, midpoint, and ending in more detail.

The Beginning Stage → Define and Initiate

The High Performance Team Coaching (HPTC) system has a strong focus on coaching teams at this beginning stage of a new task or team cycle since beginnings are critical to setting the team up for success. This "define and initiate" phase includes pre-assessment, coaching for team design, and team launch, all of which naturally benefit teams at this beginning stage.

This stage is when most of the team effectiveness conditions and framework to support success are set, which reinforces the importance of the first three coaching components to assess, define, and launch the team. This is a good time to establish ongoing team and peer coaching structures so that the team can continually engage in reflection, learning, and innovation together.

Because team coaching is most effective at team beginnings and team effectiveness is so dependent upon how teams are initially set up, it is important to try and create new beginning points for teams. Certain events can trigger a new beginning for an established team, such as the implementation of a new strategy, vision, or project, and/or some other event that reboots the team and starts it over.

The Midpoint Stage → Review and Realign

When a team is in the middle of a task or team cycle, it is critical for the team to "come up for air" to reassess, review and regain perspective. Teams naturally want to do a review at this point, so it is important for the leader or team coach to leverage and focus the team on the natural learning opportunity here. Effective coaches need to assist the team to review current processes and performance, reflect on what they have learned, and refine their strategy to best achieve their goals going forward. The coach assesses which coaching components and team effectiveness conditions are already in place and are supporting the team to be effective and which ones need improvement. We have observed that internal and external business pressures can often trigger this midpoint re-evaluation, so this is a critical time for teams and coaches to make any necessary changes.

The Ending Stage → Reassess and Integrate

Coaching in this final stage usually focuses on helping the team complete their goals and then consolidate and integrate their individual and team learning. The coach supports the team to coordinate their efforts to "make it over the finish line" and then identify factors that facilitated success, and to capture overall lessons learned. This end stage is also a time when teams may formally reassess how far they have come by identifying both the full range of outcomes they have achieved and the relationships they have developed and enhanced. The coach can assist the team to develop a plan to maintain their progress and may include a follow-up session to check back in with the team leader and/or team.

It is important to note that the end stage does not necessarily mean the team is formally ending. This stage can be simply the end of a team cycle, team project, team goal, or other set time period. Having these set time periods, especially for functional or leadership teams, can be very useful to channel the team's energy and focus. Without timeframes and milestones, teams can wander aimlessly with a lack of cohesiveness, interdependence, and urgency.

Summary

In this chapter, we highlighted the simple but important life cycle of a team, and the notion that the focus of team coaching must align appropriately to the functions that the team is performing at these beginning, middle, and end stages of its life cycle. This doesn't mean that a team has to be new or ending to do team coaching. It means that leaders and coaches need to support the team to identify natural beginnings, midpoints, and endings in their work together to keep people better focused on the start and finish lines.

The three coaching functions that match the natural beginning, midpoint, and end of a team life cycle are as follows:

1. **Define and Initiate** at the beginning of a team cycle.
2. **Review and Realign** at the midpoint.
3. **Reassess and Integrate** at the end of a team's cycle.

CHAPTER 4

Six Phases of the HPTC System

"Our coach was good in terms of being firm and bringing people back to what we were trying to accomplish. I have gone through lots of HR stuff and didn't find a whole lot of value. This was different; there were deliverables and timelines."

"Follow-up sessions were important to make sure we didn't fall back to our old ways. It was helpful because... instead of just thinking about something, we actually had to do something. Our work world is so busy, we kind of just do things, and whether we follow up is iffy. [The system] created follow up."

- Team Coaching Participants Finance Leadership Team
Multinational Corporation

Now that some of the key elements that have been proven to promote team effectiveness have been highlighted, it is time to fully review the High Performance Team Coaching (HPTC) system in detail.

There are six key phases in the HPTC system that best match the team stages (beginning, midpoint and ending) and the coaching functions that are most effective at each stage (Define and Initiate, Review and Realign, Reassess and Integrate). These six phases are outlined in Table 3, followed by Figure 4, the HPTC system "on a page." Safety is at the core of the system and is highlighted as a constant along the left side of the table. The three measures of team effectiveness, which include individual engagement, team capabilities and relationships, and quality outputs, are also identified in the table, completing the elements of the HPTC system.

Table 3:   High Performance Team Coaching System Components

	TEAM STAGE AND COACHING FUNCTION	TEAM COACHING COMPONENTS
S		1. Assessment
A	Team New Beginning → Define and Initiate	2. Coaching for Team Design
F		3. Team Launch
		4. Individual Coaching
E	Midpoint → Review and Realign	5. Ongoing Team Coaching
T	Ending → Reassess and Integrate	6. Review Learning and Successes
Y	Outcomes	Team Effectiveness • Individual Engagement • Team Capabilities and Relationships • Quality Outputs

Figure 4: The High Performance Team Coaching System on a Page
           © Peters and Carr, 2013

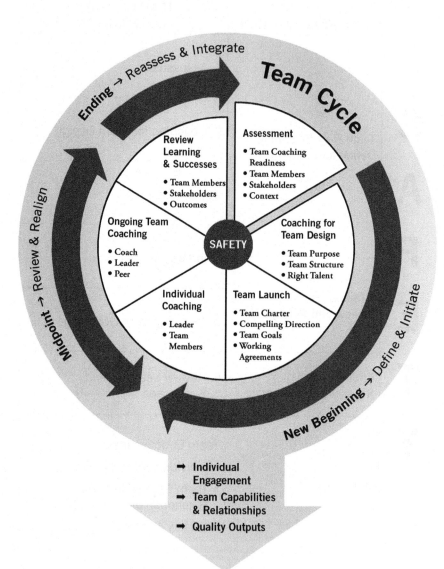

Team Effectiveness

At every stage of a team's cycle – beginning, midpoint, and ending – the High Performance Team Coaching (HPTC) system focuses on one or more of the six phases of team coaching. These stages are represented with the arrows located outside of the inner circle of the six coaching phases. However, the high performance team leader or coach may recommend that one or more phases be revisited at the team's midpoint stage, as represented by the arrow either pointing towards the team ending or its beginning phase.

For example, after assessing the team's current state, the team coach may find that it will be most effective to re-launch the team, even if the team is at a midpoint in their business, project, or life cycle. This is especially true if the team does not have clear goals, agreements, or a team charter. The goal is to create a high performance team so the coach, working closely with the team and the leader, will select and employ those strategies that are most relevant to produce the desired results.

1. Assessment

Wageman et al. (2008) outlined six key conditions for team effectiveness in their book *Senior Leadership Teams: What it takes to make them great*. These conditions are based on the factors that differentiated top performing from low and mediocre performing leadership teams around the world. Table 4 highlights these six conditions.

The assessment phase is initially aimed at determining if the team adequately meets these six conditions and other important conditions required for success, both organizationally and for team coaching. The "Team Coaching Readiness Checklist Essentials" (Carr and Peters, forthcoming in 2013) is a tangible assessment for the coach (or leader as coach) to review these important conditions for team effectiveness. A short version of this "Essentials checklist" appears later in chapter five under the assessment section.

Table 4: Essential and Enabling Conditions for High Performance Teams

ESSENTIAL CONDITIONS	ENABLING CONDITIONS
• **Real team:** defined as having clear boundaries, interdependent goals, and clarity of membership (who's on the team)	• **Solid team structure:** including clear roles and responsibilities and working agreements.
• **Compelling direction:** have a clear purpose.	• **Supportive organizational context:** information, time, money, and other resources.
• **Right people:** all team members add value to the team and have the skills and knowledge to achieve the purpose.	• **Competent team coaching:** internal or external to the team.

Source: Adapted from Wageman, et al. (2008)

Next, the coach focuses on identifying how the team is currently performing, and what the team needs to achieve in the future to be most effective and successful. Collecting this assessment information may at first appear to be time consuming and cumbersome. Think of it like starting a fitness program. It is important to have a realistic assessment of your current fitness level and your future goals to know what program to choose – are you focused on strength training, cardiovascular improvements, flexibility, or overall fitness? It is also helpful at the beginning to have a trainer do the assessment and work with you to determine the best approach given your current state and future aspirations.

This initial assessment information is ideally collected through written checklists and interviews with each team member. Leaders may choose to do the assessment themselves, however it can be helpful to have a third party complete the interviews and collect the data anonymously to allow the team members to feel safe and free to share. In addition, interviews and/or surveys with key stakeholders outside of the immediate team members can provide a broader and more systemic perspective about what the expectations for the team are from others.

At this point, a review of the organizational culture, including its characteristic style of rewards and recognition, and its reporting and decision-making expectations for the team is useful. This could include reviewing the organizational, administrative and budgetary supports for the team to understand both the scope and the constraints that the team has to make changes. At the end of the assessment phase, the team and the coach and/or leader will have information that describes team strengths, weaknesses, opportunities, and the gap between the current state and the desired future. Now the team has a direction for the next steps.

2. Coaching for Team Design

The focus areas in the second phase are well supported in the six conditions for team effectiveness outlined by Richard Hackman and Ruth Wageman in their various works on team effectiveness (Hackman, 2002; Hackman, 2012; Wageman, Hackman, and Lehman, 2005; Wageman, Nunes, Burruss, and Hackman, 2008; Wageman, Fisher, and Hackman, 2009). These six conditions were highlighted in Table 4 in the previous assessment section. The focus in this phase is to ensure that the team leader and/or team have addressed these conditions for team effectiveness, that they have defined their team purpose and goals, that they have the appropriate team structure, and that they have assigned or selected the right talent with the knowledge and skills to achieve the team's purpose and goals.

3. Team Launch

Before a team can get in the "game" it needs to know the "rules." In this third phase, the coach helps the team create or review a team charter that outlines a compelling purpose and high performance direction for the team. The team charter is discussed in greater detail in chapter five.

Working agreements are an element of the team charter that are highlighted in the HPTC system because of their key role in team effectiveness. This is backed up by our own case study research (Carr and Peters, 2012) and over a decade of experience working with teams in organizations.

Once the main team charter is drafted, the team needs to develop a common understanding and explicit working agreements that guide their work at this beginning stage. The team launch is the ideal time for this conversation. These agreements, or norms, outline how the team agrees to work and interact together to achieve the team's goals. An analogy is that the team charter outlines the "game" the team is playing and the working agreements are the "rules of the game" that tell people how to play and win together.

The working agreements help move a group of individuals from interacting in their usual ways, to being able to function optimally and more interdependently as a winning team. Blair Singer, a leadership and team specialist, said it well: "In the absence of rules, people make up their own." At the same time, safety is critical, as this quote from minister, Andy Stanley, identifies: "Rules without relationship leads to rebellion."

Finally, it is ideal if a team launch is held offsite. The session needs to be designed to build team safety and cohesion, with the goal of enhancing the team's performance and effectiveness when they get back to the office.

4. Individual Coaching

Sometimes, the team leader or individual members may need a little extra help to move the team forward. The fourth phase, individual coaching, is typically necessary for team leaders as they set the pace and framework for ensuring their team is designed well, includes the right people, and has structures to ensure people are accountable and engaged. The team leader, peers, colleagues outside of the team, or an external coach can provide this individual coaching. The best time to integrate individual coaching is at the beginning stage, as it will help a new leader set the team up for a successful start. However, individual coaching may start and/ or continue throughout the midpoint and even ending of a team cycle.

Individual coaching is not limited to the team leader in the HPTC system. Other team members may benefit from individual coaching to support their development and skill building too. The goal of individual coaching in the HPTC system is to challenge and develop team members to contribute and interact as effectively as possible on the team. Chapter five outlines some questions to help determine if individual coaching may be a beneficial adjunct to support the team's performance.

5. Ongoing Team Coaching

Ongoing or follow-up team coaching sessions reinforce and further the team's agreements and actions. If the team has had an external coach up until this point, the team leader may start to take on more coaching of the team in this phase. Additionally, as early as the team launch, the coach may train the team members and/or set up peer coaching supports to ensure that individual change continues to occur after the launch, back in the workplace. Peer coaching can also support team accountability and helps the team strengthen its cohesion and intrapersonal network. In fact, peer coaching and peer feedback are increasingly seen as key drivers of employee engagement, according to surveys done by the Corporate Leadership Council (2011).

6. Review Learning and Successes

After any team project, it is important to take the time to review successes and any lessons learned. This is the goal of the final phase of the HPTC system, when team members are urged to reflect upon and capture their learning at the end of a team cycle. The team coach's role at the end stage of a team's cycle is to facilitate the team's learning, and to integrate its review of the tasks, project, milestones, or even formal team ending. This is a critical stage that is often missed or given little attention. Although highlighted as the final phase of the system, it is important for leaders and coaches to remember to support team learning at all stages of their development. Many team coaching and team effectiveness practitioners emphasize that teams need to consciously decide upon and implement a process that encourages learning and continuous improvement (Clutterbuck, 2007; Hawkins, 2011; Hackman, 2003).

Summary

This chapter presented the full High Performance Team Coaching system, along with an overview of the key research that underpins the system. The six HPTC phases are:

1. Assessment
2. Coaching for Team Design
3. Team Launch
4. Individual Coaching
5. Ongoing Team Coaching
6. Review of Learning and Successes

Remember that safety is the glue that holds the entire system together and leads to the three outcomes that exemplify high performance teams: individual engagement, team capabilities and relationships, and quality outputs.

> **In the absence of rules, people make up their own.**
> - Blair Singer, Author and CEO
> **BUT**
> **Rules without relationship leads to rebellion.**
> - Andy Stanley, Minister

CHAPTER 5

Activities to Support the Six Phases

"People got engaged doing the team charter and those activities [that the team coach introduced.] I thought that an activity, whether it was a game or not, helped us to see things differently."

- Team member, Corporate Finance Leadership Team

This section highlights some sample activities and tools to implement the HPTC system. These activities and tools are particularly useful for the team leader, an HR manager, or any internal or external team coach. These activities represent only a sampling of the essential components of the HPTC programs that we implement with our clients. There are many other activities, tools and strategies that could be implemented for each phase, based on the needs of the particular time. To get started, this chapter overviews a few tools and techniques that we have found to be particularly useful. The suggested activities and checklists also provide a practical roadmap for planning a team coaching approach.

Note that although the six phases are presented in a linear fashion, not all phases of the High Performance Team Coaching system happen independently and are neatly completed before the next phase begins. There is often overlap occurring. A skilled leader or coach navigates between the phases according to what the team needs, and keeps all six areas in mind throughout the coaching.

1. Assessment

Assessment in the HPTC system is aimed at identifying if the six conditions for team effectiveness, outlined in chapter three, are adequately in place. Assessment is best facilitated by someone external to the team, even if the team leader will be doing the ongoing team coaching. External assessment facilitates a feeling of safety at this very important phase.

As a reminder, the first five conditions to establish include:

1. Defining a real team.
2. Creating a compelling direction and purpose.
3. Having the right people with the right knowledge and skills.
4. Creating a solid team structure.
5. Ensuring a supportive organizational context.

Once these five effectiveness conditions are addressed at a sufficient level, then the sixth condition for team effectiveness, competent team coaching, can start on a solid foundation.

The following "Team Coaching Readiness Assessment" is a helpful tool for coaches and leaders to identify if the team's design and structure is appropriate for coaching to occur. The goal is to have more positive or "yes" answers than negative or "no" answers on the assessment. However, it is not a black and white diagnostic tool. Rather, it is a guide for reflection and discussion to ensure that the team is set up for success.

If there are conditions that are uncovered by the assessment that could be major impediments to the team's success, then a coach can support the team leader by clarifying problematic conditions and creating a plan to address these. In this case, the assessment would have mostly "no" answers to the questions, and the team structure and design would benefit from further development and support. These structure and design changes would be best accomplished through team leader coaching first, before beginning any whole team coaching.

Team Coaching Readiness Assessment

☐ Does everyone know and agree on who is on the team?

☐ Do you have the right number of team members that you need – no more and no less? Several researchers have indicated that five to 10 members is the ideal team size.

☐ Do you have the best mix of team members (knowledge, skills, talent) to achieve the team purpose?

☐ Do you expect the team membership to be relatively stable during the team coaching period?

☐ Do you have a compelling purpose for the team?

☐ Do you have goals that require all team members to participate in their success?

☐ Does the team meet regularly?

☐ Are there any team members who have performance issues that need to be addressed first or separately?

☐ Does the team have the resources required to achieve their goals?
    ☐ Time
    ☐ Money
    ☐ Information

☐ Does the team have clear working agreements / norms for how people work together?

☐ How motivated is the leader to engage in team coaching (low to high)?
    ☐ Not engaged
    ☐ Somewhat engaged
    ☐ Highly engaged

☐ How motivated are team members to engage in team coaching?

☐ Is there support from the leadership outside of the team (i.e., the leader's leader) to engage in team coaching?

☐ Is the team able and willing to dedicate time to achieve the coaching goals?

☐ Does the team know how to define and/or measure success?

☐ Are there potential obstacles that might get in the way of the team participating in coaching? If so, what are they?

Reviewing and addressing these coaching readiness factors is critical. Starting team coaching without these factors in place can lead to failure (Wageman, Fisher and Hackman, 2009). It may feel good and even expedient to just dive in with coaching or to start a conversation about group dynamics with a team. However, your efforts will be like putting new paint over an unprimed wall… it won't be long before the paint starts to peel.

Introductory Team Coaching Overview Session

If the team coaching readiness factors and the team design are adequate, then the leader or coach meets with the team to provide the team coaching overview. The coach offers a clear orientation to the team coaching process in this session, in order to generate interest and engagement. The coach reviews all the steps, roles, and responsibilities. It is important to ensure team members understand what team coaching is, what the coaching entails, and why coaching will be helpful.

Team Member Interviews

Next, the coach conducts individual interviews with team members and relevant stakeholders to identify their team strengths, weaknesses, challenges and opportunities. The Pre-Coaching Team Member Interview Guide identifies some potential questions to ask. Potential stakeholder interviewees could include colleagues, suppliers, senior leaders, or customers. The coach also needs to review relevant documents and information to better discuss the organizational context with the leader and team.

There are a variety of commercially available team assessments that could provide further insight into the team's dynamics and effectiveness, including the forthcoming High Performance Team Coaching Assessment (Peters, forthcoming in 2013). Coaches may also choose to

Pre-Coaching Team Member Interview Guide

☐ What does your team need to be doing to be successful a year from now?

☐ What do your stakeholders (e.g., customers, suppliers, executive team, the board, other internal teams) need most from this team?

☐ What do you see as your team's top three strengths?

☐ What two things could your team do differently to be even more effective?

☐ What conversations does your team avoid that would be beneficial to explore if you could do this in a safe manner?

☐ On a scale of 1 to 10 (low to high), how would you rate this team's overall effectiveness?

☐ What key factors influenced your rating?

☐ What would you most like the team coaching to address?

☐ How will you measure success of the team coaching?

☐ What other comments do you have about your team's current functioning and effectiveness?

use a personality or behavioural style assessment to augment the team's knowledge about each other, as teams generally find the results informative and insightful. There are many commercial style assessments available, such as the Myers-Briggs Type Indicator, DISC, and Insights.

Reviewing the Team Assessments

Once the assessments are complete, the team coach compiles an assessment report that provides a full, anonymous summary of the pre-coaching assessment data. No comments should be linked to any one team member. This report does not identify the themes and provide conclusions; it just organizes the information clearly and succinctly so that the team can analyze and come to their own conclusions about themes. The focus is on coaching the team to look at the report as objective observers who come to their own insights and ownership of the team's current state. This is distinctly different from a consulting approach, which would be focused on the coach or consultant providing conclusions and recommendations to the team.

To ensure that a discussion of the results occurs, the team coach facilitates a pre-coaching debrief meeting for the team to review the assessment reports. At this point, they identify for themselves themes in their strengths, weaknesses, challenges, and outcomes. The team reviews what they are hearing and seeing and determines their next steps to be successful. Although it is tempting to do it for them, do not jump in and interpret the findings for the team. Let them interpret the results for themselves. This way the team owns their own challenges and opportunities, and this makes them more likely to follow through on new commitments arising out of the assessment findings and coaching.

At the end of the discussion, collaborate with the team to help them come to agreement about some high-level goals and an overall direction for the coaching. Some key principles and questions that help to assess if the team coaching goals will be impactful are listed below.

Assessing Team Coaching Goals

☐ Are the goals clear?

☐ Are the goals consequential and connected to the team's strategic objectives?

☐ Can you measure the goals?

☐ Do team members need to rely on one another to accomplish the goals?

☐ Are people committed to achieving them?

☐ Can you get started on the goals right away?

Finally, use this initial time with the team to identify measures of success at the end of the coaching period. Help them identify what they want to achieve, and how they will know they have been successful. Ensure that their goals are measurable, include business results, and that everyone is clear about the meaning of each goal.

2. Coaching for Team Design

Based on the assessment, determine if the necessary conditions and supports are in place to begin team coaching, starting with the team launch (phase 3). If the conditions are not well established, coach the leader to establish an appropriate structure, design and conditions that will support team effectiveness, since a strong structure and design is responsible for 60 per cent of any team's success.

Many teams experience interpersonal issues and these are often the reason external team coaches are hired. Sometimes these problems can be the result of structure and design issues, such as unclear roles and responsibilities or a lack of working agreements (Beckhard, 1972). Review the structure and design first before assuming there is an interpersonal problem. The previous "Team Coaching Readiness Assessment" is a useful tool to identify any conditions that need to be addressed or strengthened. Remember, without the right team design, coaching is unlikely to succeed.

An external coach might want to take a more consultative approach at this stage. This means working with the team leader to identify and make changes to the team design that are impeding progress, rather than inappropriately applying coaching to solve a performance issue or structural flaw.

In the end, it is a judgement call whether or not to proceed to the next phase of the HPTC system, the team launch. Consider the following:

- What is the risk of proceeding with coaching if most of the team effectiveness conditions are not addressed?

- How much progress do you think you can make if you start now? If you wait?
- What is the risk of waiting to start the team coaching versus resolving the team design issues first?

Teams are dynamic and always changing, which makes it even more important to ensure that the team is well set up to succeed. A properly designed team that has effective structures and norms allows for greater agility and, when needed, better integration of new members, fostering continued success.

3. Team Launch

The team launch is an opportunity to focus on setting the stage for change. It is important to create a safe, reflective space for the team to think deeply about their current and desired state, and to create alignment between personal and team goals. This is usually a two-day, or at least a one-day session with all of the team members present.

It is highly recommended that this session be held away from the team's usual workplace to minimize interruptions and allow for more comfort and safety. Being offsite also supports concentrated time together and facilitates opportunities to interact in less formal and sometimes more authentic ways.

The team launch can be an ideal time to debrief a personality or behavioural style assessment if one was used during the assessment phase. Support the team to look not only at understanding their own individual styles, but also the implications to the team's overall style profile. How could their team profile influence how they work together? Discuss how others may perceive them as a team, and how their individual and team profiles affect their ability to achieve their business goals.

- What does that team need to keep front of mind about their profile?

- What team strengths are being over-used or under-used?
- In which ways are people over-adapting to fit their environment?

Team Charter

One of the key outcomes from the team launch is a team charter. This document includes important components such as vision, mission, values, goals, strategies, success measures, and most importantly, team working agreements. Ideally, this is a one-page summary for the team to quickly see what they are set to do, how they will do it, and how they will know when they have been successful. The team charter can be useful for sharing with other stakeholders and/or for integrating new team members. A sample of a Team Charter on a Page is provided in Figure 5.

When developing a team charter, note that team vision and mission are often misunderstood. Vision statements explain WHY an organization or team is doing that work and frames the ideal future to which it aspires. The vision provides a vivid, idealized future that inspires and energizes people to achieve a greater purpose in their work. Vision statements create a mental picture of a target or goal. It raises the level of excellence and establishes meaning today and hope for tomorrow, which is critical in employee engagement. Sample questions to help define a team vision statement include:

Vision Statement Questions

☐ What do we want to be?

☐ What is our dream or vision?

☐ What makes our area unique or distinctive?

☐ What excellence or special expertise is offered?

☐ What sets us apart?

☐ What is our measure of success?

☐ What do we offer that will make a difference?

Vision Statement Examples

Microsoft

"Our vision drives everything we do: A computer on every desk and in every home using great software as an empowering tool."

Compaq

"To be the leading supplier of PCs and PC servers in all customer segments."

McDonald's

"To be the world's best quick service restaurant experience."

Walt Disney Company

"To be one of the world's leading producers and providers of entertainment and information."

Any team can articulate their own vision statement; they don't have to just use the organization's vision, although their team vision will need to support the organization's overall vision. For example, a leadership team for a finance department had a vision to "provide financial solutions to support organizational growth and success." The organization they were in was focused on growth through acquisition. Another example is a human resources leadership team that defined their vision to be "a sustainable, best in class HR department that supports the talent acquisition, development, and engagement of our people." And at a broader level, an organization's leadership team may have a vision to "lead and grow the talent in the organization to meet their stakeholder requirements and achieve their key goals."

Remember that the vision is not the end itself, but a guiding force for the team. It does set the stage for greatness, but it is insufficient on its own. There is a Japanese proverb that says: "Vision without action is a daydream and action without vision is a nightmare." Ensure that at the end of the team charter discussion there are goals and actions to support the team to implement the vision.

Figure 5: Team Charter on a Page

TEAM CHARTER for TEAM NAME DATE		
Vision		
Team Mission or Mandate or Purpose		
Team Members	**Working Agreements**	**Key Goals**
Values		**Success Measures**

Mission statements are less lofty than vision statements. Mission statements tell WHAT the organization or team does to achieve that vision. The mission statement describes who the team is, why it exists, as well as what it does. It defines the business the team or organization is in. By describing clearly in a simple statement or two, the mission gets everyone on the same path, makes decision making easier, creates common expectations, helps employees focus better, and ultimately helps customers find you easily. If you serve the internal organization, it helps your clients or internal customers know what to expect from you.

Mission Statement Examples

McDonald's

"Being the best means providing outstanding quality, service, cleanliness, and value, so that we make every customer in every restaurant smile."

Walt Disney Company

"Using our portfolio of brands to differentiate our content, services and consumer products, we seek to develop the most creative, innovative and profitable entertainment experiences and related products in the world."

FedEx

Produce superior financial returns for shareowners by providing high value-added supply chain, transportation, business and related information services through focused operating companies. Customer requirements will be met in the highest quality manner appropriate to each market segment served. FedEx will strive to develop mutually rewarding relationships with its employees, partners and suppliers. Safety will be the first consideration in all operations. Corporate activities will be conducted to the highest ethical and professional standards."

Google

"To organize the world's information and make it universally accessible and useful."

Creating vision and mission statements is moʹ
lectual exercise. Companies whose employees understaι.
and goals enjoy on average a 29 per cent greater return than otɦϲ
(Watson Wyatt Work Study, 2008). Thus, they form an important parι
of any team charter and help define the rest of the charter components.

Working Agreements

A key component of the team charter is to set clear working agreements. Craft a list of three to eight working agreements that details how the team needs to work together to achieve their vision, purpose, and the goals. Too many agreements can become burdensome to implement. Working agreements should include how the team will hold themselves and each other accountable to the agreements, and what to do when any agreements are broken. Make a point of encouraging team members to assume good intentions, which can create a safer and gentler way for colleagues to call out broken agreements.

To begin defining agreements or norms for the team, ask team members to think about their meetings, decisions, communication, reporting, roles and responsibilities in the team, etc. Some sample questions follow.

Questions for Defining Working Agreements

- ☐ What will it take for us to achieve significant performance results?
- ☐ How do we currently work together in ways that help us move towards even higher performance?
- ☐ What recurring issues repeatedly interfere with our performance?
- ☐ What enhances my own engagement and performance on the team?
- ☐ What behaviours shut me down?
- ☐ What key agreements would we need to follow in the team to reach our goals?

Working Agreement Examples

- Listen to understand, not respond.
- Be honest.
- Respect everyone's knowledge and experience.
- Share information with each other, but let people know if information is confidential.
- Pay attention to body language / social signs.
- Speak up when your needs are not met.
- Stay curious.
- Get input and hear everyone's ideas first before diving into the task.
- Accept failures with the courage to forgive and move on.
- Make a decision by consensus if possible, with a fall back process of a majority vote for input, which will lead to a compromise or unilateral decision by the key owner of the decision.

Working agreements are just that – working. They do no good sitting on a shelf or in a file. Make the agreements active by posting them for every meeting and in conspicuous places where the team works so that they can hold each other and themselves accountable. Hold a team discussion about how the working agreements are "working" at regular intervals, such as every second or third meeting.

Business Measures and Outcomes

It is ideal for teams to identify clear business measures and outcomes for themselves as a result of the coaching. Ask the team:

- What business measures will the team track and measure to assess if overall performance and effectiveness are improving?
- What do stakeholders need the team to be doing differently in a year's time?
- What is the risk if the team does not aim for this change?
- What is the possible payoff if the team does take the risk?

4. Individual Coaching

Individual coaching of the team leader is a powerful and helpful adjunct to the team level coaching. Even if the team leader is acting as the team coach, providing coaching to the team leader can deepen their coaching skills and improve their ability to lead an effective team culture. Individual coaching can also allow the team leader to reflect upon the team in a safer and more neutral way, allowing for reflection and a strategic review of the team's progress and next steps.

If the leader is not acting as the team coach, individual coaching can help the leader transition to become the team coach in the future and to sustain change. Even while engaging an external coach, the leader can help with many team coaching elements including:

- Implementing the coaching agreements and actions to ensure the team's success.
- Working with the coach to create leadership goals that align with the team goals.
- Collaborating with the coach so that the leader fully participates in the planning and facilitation of the team coaching sessions.
- Observing the coaching skills modelled by the coach so the leader can learn how to coach individuals and the team better in between sessions.
- Eventually taking over the ongoing coaching of the team.

A team coach who is external to the team can help the leader understand how his or her leadership behaviour is crucial to how the team performs and the quality of the business results achieved. Without objective, external guidance, leaders who take on the team coach role may have a hard time seeing their own behaviour and contributions to team dynamics clearly.

Individual team members can also benefit from individual coaching. Team coaches can provide individual coaching if desired or necessary to support the achievement of individual goals that align with team goals. Coaching can be especially helpful for team members who are informal leaders in the team and strong influencers of team behaviour. It can also support a team member who needs to learn how to better participate in or influence the team.

If only one or a few team members are selected to receive individual coaching, it is important for the leader and the coach to be clear about the rationale for their decision. This means discussing the purpose and goals with the team member(s) identified for the individual coaching. It may or may not be appropriate to disclose to the team that any one individual is receiving adjunct coaching. The team leader will need to make a decision about this with the best interests of the team and the individual in mind.

The end goal of both individual and team coaching is to achieve a well-designed team with productive team meetings that encourage and allow everyone to contribute. It is important for all members on a team to provide their specialized knowledge effectively, and not to overshadow the contributions of their fellow team members in the process. In essence, individual coaching can help team members think about what they can do and how they need to interact with their team to help everyone succeed.

5. Ongoing Team Coaching

Ongoing team coaching is required on a monthly or quarterly basis, and is dependent on how long the team has to achieve its goals and how much support the team needs to do so. These sessions need to focus on supporting the team to follow through on their team charter, which includes their working agreements, goals, and the actions the team agreed to move forward. Provide coaching around team dynamics only when team member interactions start to impede progress on the team's collective work together.

There is some compelling early research by Richard Beckhard (1972), and Hackman and Wageman (2005) that indicated that working on interpersonal dynamics for interpersonal dynamics sake is rarely effective. Human nature dictates that most of us are primed to see these interpersonal issues rather than the underlying structures and team design elements that are the real issues. Astute team coaches are constantly on the lookout for these red herrings when they are called on to "fix the team dynamics."

Focusing on "positive signs of success" is also important. A strong focus on success has been linked to greater individual and team achievement, especially in the fields of sports psychology and positive psychology. In practice, this means taking the time to ask the team about what is going well and what is new and promising. On very troubled, but well-designed teams, it can be helpful to ask team members to name one time that the team interacted in a positive way together. Then ask them if this were to occur more often, how would it make a difference to their interactions and results?

Ongoing coaching can also help build safety and trust by using techniques such as check-ins about team member thoughts and feelings at the beginning and end of sessions. This can help surface sensitive issues. Coaching sessions can also promote accountability by asking how the team is doing with staying true and aligned to their working agreements and goals.

Ongoing team coaching often involves attending some of the team's regular meetings or booking specific meetings for coaching. Here are six specific techniques to use in ongoing coaching sessions:

1. **Live action coaching.** Remember the working agreements? Are team members sticking to them or not? Offer feedback or coaching questions that will immediately let them move towards a new way of working together. Remind team members to take note of

the process of their meetings - "how" they are working together during meetings, not just "what" they are talking about.

2. **Success check-ins.** It is easy to focus on issues and problems. Reinforce success by asking team members to check in on small signs of change or small wins they notice since the last time they met together.

3. **Stay real.** It's easy for teams to fall back into their usual roles and ways of interacting with one another, which can include not addressing differences of opinion or conflict, or not ensuring everyone has a voice in the room. What dysfunctional patterns like this are apparent? Does the team notice these patterns themselves?

4. **Team huddle.** Halfway through the meeting invite team members to pause and comment on one thing that is going well and one thing that could be changed to improve their meetings. Without responding to what each person said, carry on with the meeting. Often this kind of team huddle creates powerful change all by itself. Reinforce this as an ongoing activity for the team in their meetings.

5. **Round robins.** How can the team draw on its resources and strengths even more, both during and between meetings? One way to do this is to ensure that the coach actively asks for comments and participation from everyone. Asking for round robin comments with equal time for all members to talk is a tried and true technique for ensuring participation.

6. **Divide and conquer.** One way to ensure that meetings stay on track is to assign team members to take on different roles in the meeting (facilitator, note taker, time keeper, etc.). This builds structure and accountability for the team to better manage their own team meetings when a facilitator, leader, or team coach is not present.

The GROUP Model for Team Coaching Sessions

Saul Brown and Anthony Grant (2010), two coaching researchers and practitioners, developed a useful model for managing team conversations Their model is called GROUP which is an acronym that stands for Goal, Reality, Options, Understand Others, and Perform. Highlights of what to do in each stage of this model is provided in the GROUP Question Guide.

GROUP Question Guide

☐ **Goal:** Ask the group what they want to achieve during this meeting or coaching session.

☐ **Reality:** Ask the group to review what realities are impacting their goals, including factors that might be facilitating their success and factors that might be inhibiting their success or ability to achieve success.

☐ **Options:** Help the group to identify, consider, and assess options to achieve their goals. This includes brainstorming and reviews of what has and has not worked in the past.

☐ **Understand Others:** The coach supports the team to observe and reflect upon their own individual reactions and responses to what is going on and being said in the group. Encourage team members to focus on exploring others' perspectives through questions and a few minutes of individual reflection during the meeting.

☐ **Perform:** Finally, the team coach helps the team identify actions and next steps to take to support the team's goals and plans. Ensure the team is clear about the accountability of action items, marking dates and names next to each action. Support them to imagine their success and to identify potential roadblocks that they will need to overcome to achieve success.

Source: Adapted from Brown and Grant, 2010:38

Peer Coaching

Peer coaching has been occurring informally and formally in organizations for decades. Colleagues regularly discuss issues and provide each other with mutual support through brainstorming, problem solving and by acting as a sounding board. So what is different about peer coaching in the HPTC system? It is formally encouraged as a way for team members to interact on a regular basis. For instance, in response to situations where gossiping or complaining would be more the norm, or to support one another to make sense of their work goals.

> Reciprocal peer coaching occurs where peers take turns voluntarily to coach each other, so that each has an opportunity to receive valuable coaching on their own agenda from an equally experienced and trusted peer.
> (Cox, 2012:429)

Elaine Cox, a coaching practitioner, researcher, and author aptly highlights the value of peer coaching. She says, 'peer coaching taps into a source of less costly, in-house expertise, and support that is highly relevant and readily available in the workplace" (Cox, 2012, p. 428). Peer coaching is not just an inexpensive personal development tool for organizations, though. It can be a key lever to support the ongoing coaching and development of the team as an adjunct to the coaching provided by the leader or team coach. However, effective peer coaching may not happen on its own without strong modeling and support.

Through our work with teams, we have found that it's important to create a framework for peer coaching that may include specifying confidentiality agreements that help build safety and trust, and providing explicit permission for peers to coach each other. Support may also include training the team in coaching skills, since many peer conversations may not naturally be coaching conversations. The GROUP model presented in the previous section could also be used as the framework for these individual coaching conversations. As noted earlier, GROUP expands upon the GROW model (Goal, Reality, Options, and Way forward) by adding on the concepts of understanding one another and performing as a team. These latter two steps are perfect for maintaining the dual focus in a peer coaching conversation on the individual being coached and the larger team context.

So how important is peer coaching as a strategy in the HPTC system? Hackman and O'Connor (2005) found that peer coaching was one of the most powerful team development activities that team members could use to create and maintain team performance. Further, the amount and quality of peer coaching and peer feedback is becoming more and more important as a method to increase engagement in organizations (Corporate Leadership Council, 2011). Some of the areas that the Corporate Leadership Council found where peer coaching and feedback were most important for team engagement were:

- Helping each other translate goals into day-to-day work.
- Providing informal feedback.
- Providing career path information to one another.

In reviewing the list, it's clear that the value colleagues provide to each other's engagement is not just achieved from hanging out or attending social events together on a regular basis. It really is about how peers and colleagues provide safe, deliberate, meaningful, and skillful support to each other in order to help achieve their mutual and independent goals.

Additional support for peer coaching was found in our own team coaching research when team members talked about the outcomes they derived from peer coaching. Team members indicated results such as:

- Supporting each other to have difficult conversations that are needed with other team members.

- Helping one another stay positive and motivated by supporting each other's ideas and encouraging one another.
- Offering feedback about behaviours that contradict the working agreements.

Overall, employees indicate that they experience great value and support when trusted colleagues provide informal feedback and when they help translate corporate goals into everyday work activities. These are two important ways that peer coaching can help drive results and engagement. Team members benefit from informally and formally coaching each other and coaching the team as a whole, especially between meetings or when the team coach or leader is not present. To be most successful, formal training and working agreements about peer coaching are helpful to give team members the skills and permission to effectively help one another achieve their goals.

6. Review Learning and Successes

Reviewing learning and successes is structured as the final phase of the HPTC system, however, reviews are also important throughout the business cycle and team coaching. Teams need to take time to reflect on what they are learning and the successes they achieve during their work together, especially at the end of a team project or business cycle. This review of learning and successes is not something teams tend to build in nor effectively do on their own without external guidance (Hackman, 2003). Coaches can invite teams to pause, consider, and integrate meta-level insights throughout the coaching.

In the final coaching sessions of the HPTC system, reviewing learning and successes, team coaches can use a similar format to the pre-coaching assessment phase. This usually means re-doing the assessments that were completed at the beginning of the coaching. This may include optional interviews with team members and stakeholders, as well as re-doing any team assessments the team did to identify business or team performance. It is typically not necessary or advised to redo the style assessment, if one was completed initially. Style assessment data and information is best integrated and discussed throughout the coaching as it relates to how the team is working together.

The coach compiles and summarizes the post-coaching assessment data and feedback to share with the team. Then the coach debriefs the post-coaching assessments with the team by once again having them collectively review the information and identify for themselves the themes they notice. The focus is on learning and identifying tangible outcomes that the team has achieved. Again, it is critical as a team coach not to provide conclusions, recommendations, or do the team's analysis for them. This would move the coach firmly into a consultant role and would take ownership and accountability away from the team.

Use a formal coaching review session to encourage and celebrate team success. Ask the team what they notice is different about their team now versus when they started. What did they achieve together that they could not have achieved alone? What did they learn about themselves and their team that enables them to work better together now and in the future? If your team responds to creative exercises, ask them what the team coaching journey would look like as a metaphor, a novel, or a song.

Even if the team did not achieve all their goals or is still working towards their final milestone, a focus on successes and strengths will help the team better understand what they do well and how to do more of that in the future.

At the final coaching session, it can be helpful to obtain agreement from the team if they would like any external coaching for sustainment or follow-up to support them as they move into either a maintenance or a new beginning stage. Review what their original measures of success were and identify what they achieved through the coaching. Discuss what they learned and have implemented in the coaching and how they can continue to apply this learning and new skills to current team realities. Ask them who will take on the team coaching role and/or pay attention to how the team is working together in the future. Have them identify a structure for continuing to learn and grow. Encourage the team leader to set up a follow-up call or team session to refresh the team's motivation to continually develop and succeed.

Learning and Success Review Questions

☐ What is different about your team now that you have completed this period of team coaching?

☐ What do you see as your team's top three strengths now?

☐ What would others who are important to the team and/or rely on your team's work say about your team?

☐ On a scale of 1 to 10 (low to high), how would you rate this team's overall effectiveness now?

☐ What key factors influenced your rating?

☐ What two things could your team do to continue to move forward?

☐ List your team's measures of success. On a scale of 1 to 10, how did your team do in meeting the target(s)?

☐ What other comments do you have about your team's current functioning and effectiveness?

☐ Do you have any feedback on what was most beneficial from the team coaching? Least beneficial?

Learning Dialogues

It is important for the team not only to review its performance and successes of the team at the end of a team cycle, but also to build its members' capacity to learn together throughout their time working together. It might seem like the team does not have the time to participate in a learning dialogue, but doing so will save time in the long run as the team improves together.

Be sure to fully engage all team members during these learning and review conversations. It can also be helpful to schedule learning dialogues on a regular basis (e.g., bi-monthly or quarterly) to keep the team developing and focused on continuous improvement at all stages of a team or business cycle.

Learning Dialogue Questions

☐ What did we learn about how we learn?

☐ What have we learned this month / quarter / year as a team that was most useful to us?

☐ How do we keep that going?

☐ What did we learn that was most surprising?

☐ If we had to advise a team like ours, given what we know now, what would we say is most important for them to keep in mind?

☐ What did we talk about changing but did not change? What will change this pattern?

☐ What can we celebrate about our work together? How can we build on these successes?

Summary

There are many activities that can support the six phases of the High Performance Team Coaching system. This chapter highlights a few ideas and options to get started. It is important to be clear about the starting point for a team and what is driving the leader or coach to begin the coaching at that point. Although it is possible to implement only certain phases of the HPTC system, the most effective approach is to carry out all six of the researched phases together to foster lasting change for teams. Ideally, begin with assisting a new team at its formation, or create a new starting point with an already formed team by coaching them around a new strategy, project, or change initiative.

Abbreviating the team coaching process can be like taking an antibiotic for only five days when you need seven days. You think you are better, but your body really needs those extra days to fully recover. Ideally the external team coach, or the team leader as coach, will support the team through the full team cycle, including follow-up, to ensure the greatest effectiveness and success for the current goals and the long term performance of the team and its members.

CHAPTER 6

Five Tips for
Transforming Teams

"So we all went in [to the team coaching] with an open mind [to transform our team] and I'm overwhelmed and delighted with what happened. There was more that came out than I thought was even possible. I think it was because we were all so committed to it. And maybe there were some uncomfortable moments, but that's part of growth."

- Team member of a Senior Leadership Team
Major Government Department

This chapter is a bonus chapter that previews five tips from the companion book, *50 Tips for Terrific Teams* (Peters and Carr, 2013).

These extra tips also support teams to be more effective and may be implemented either within or independent of the High Performance Team Coaching system. Using even one of these five tips will enhance your team's performance. Pay special attention to Tip #2: Take turns to leverage your collective intelligence. Although it appears to be a simple reminder, are you really doing it as a team? Following basic turn-taking principles has been proven to make a significant difference to team effectiveness.

TIP #1: Use your experts effectively.

Typically, **experts** need help to be effective team contributors because:

> The presence of expert members may actually decrease team effectiveness if members are not helped to use the experts' special talents.
> (Woolley et al., 2008:16)

Do not assume that because there is an expert (someone with appreciably higher knowledge or skill) on the team that this expert person will inevitably contribute to increased team performance. In fact, the opposite is likely true. Experts may pay less attention to others' contributions and others may give too much credence to expert views. It is equally important to have team members with breadth of experience and strong interpersonal skills to help ensure everyone's input is considered. It is not always possible to decide who is on the team though, so ensure that there are structures in place so that everyone contributes, and that experts do not dominate the conversations.

ACTIONS

1. Think twice before you put the expert in charge. Their expertise is valuable, however, knowledge and technical skills do not necessarily equate to leadership skills. Assess for these skills separately.
2. Include members with a diversity of skills and abilities that contribute to achieving the goal or task.
3. Ensure that everyone's role and style is recognized as important for achieving your team's goals.
4. Provide explicit instructions and confirm agreements about how members will carry out their joint work together. Don't assume this will happen naturally.

TIP #2: Take turns to leverage your collective intelligence.

> Groups where a few people dominated the
> conversation were less collectively intelligent
> than those with a more equal distribution
> of conversational turn-taking.
> (Woolley et al., 2010:688)

We cannot raise individual intelligence, but we can increase the collective intelligence of a team where the sum is truly greater than the parts. To do this, ensure that the team uses processes that not only encourage, but also **require everyone to participate**. Use "brainsteering", a technique to ensure you get as many individual ideas as possible and minimize groupthink by asking the right questions and allowing people to reflect on their own before contributing as a group—your reflective introverts will appreciate this (Coyne and Coyne, 2011)!

ACTIONS

To implement brainsteering, follow these steps:

1. Give everyone time before a meeting and/or a few minutes during a meeting to reflect on the issue or question to be discussed.
2. Ask focused questions that invite people to look at the challenge from a different or more specific angle than you have before.
3. Give all team members an equal chance to share their thoughts in a round robin conversation style or email exchange.
4. Tell people, "Even if you think you are being redundant, say it in your own words." Often some unique slant or perspective is revealed from this approach.
5. Ensure that everyone has similar time or space to contribute.
6. Acknowledge everyone's contribution or comment with a simple "thank you" so that nobody's comments are given more weight or value than others.

TIP #3: Collaborate to save time and costs.

> If the collaboration efficiency of only 20
> of the less efficient project managers and
> organizational leaders improved from
> below-average to average, it would save
> the roughly 400 individuals who interacted
> regularly with those managers and leaders
> up to 1,500 hours per week.
> - Results of a six-year organizational study
> (Cross et al, 2010)

Formal accountability structures are important but they are not enough in today's innovative and intersecting teams and companies. It is these informal **collaboration** networks and spontaneous interactions between people who see problems from different perspectives that are helpful. What's more, people often draw on their networks to successfully execute plans, particularly when the path to success is not obvious or becomes more complicated than expected.

ACTIONS

1. Create opportunities across teams to foster networking, collaboration and innovation.
2. Identify explicit working agreements that foster collaboration.
3. Ask team members to seek input from inside and outside the team and set up a time and structure to share that information in the team. Ask each member to connect with someone outside of their usual circle; this approach will invite and allow more innovative ideas to surface.
4. Experiment together and allow for testing and revisiting of new ideas and approaches.

TIP #4: Shift your thinking from indifferent to empathetic.

> Before we can truly understand another person,
> we must walk a mile in their moccasins.
> Before we can walk in their moccasins,
> we must take off our own.
> - Native American Proverb

Pate and Shoblom (2013) have identified a technique that allows individuals to effectively shift their thinking from **indifferent to empathetic**, especially when there is high conflict among team members that causes people to disengage. Indifference, or apathy, is counter-productive to effective team performance. In contrast, empathy is a key behaviour of effective team members (Wageman et al., 2008). To avoid apathy, challenge assumptions, clarify values and priorities, and expand the set of viable action steps. This can decrease indifference and increase the likelihood of empathetic behaviour in teams.

ACTIONS

Try these three techniques to shift the team's conversational style, starting with your own style.

1. Challenge your own assumptions about what you are thinking or doing. Ask: "How do I know this is true?"

2. Be aware of values, concerns and priorities for different individuals. Consider: "What do I know is important to this person? Given this, how does their position make sense?"

3. Identify possible courses of action. Ask: "What other possibilities exist here and are inclusive of what we collectively want?"

TIP #5: Make five times more positive than negative comments.

The highest performing teams have interactions with at least five times more (5.8 to 1) **positive than negative comments** and affirming body language signals (Frederickson and Losada, 2005). These higher performance business teams not only demonstrate greater positivity towards each other, they also have higher profitability, better customer satisfaction scores, and higher evaluations from others in the organization.

Interestingly enough, John Gottman (1994), a prolific writer and researcher on successful couples, also found that the same ratios predicted the success or demise of relationships. The most successful couples demonstrated the same 5 to 1 positive to negative ratio, even when in conflict. In fact, 2.9 is the "Losada Line", or the ratio of positivity to negativity that separates teams and individuals who succeed from those who are less effective.

ACTIONS

1. Bring in an independent observer to your team meeting OR observe it yourself when another team member is chairing the team meeting. Have the observer track the number of positive and negative comments and body language signals.

2. When debriefing the results, ensure your team understands the financial and stakeholder satisfaction benefits of expressing positivity and ask: "How can we foster a more positive environment?"

3. Begin your remarks by commenting on the positive to model receptivity.

4. Don't over-do the positive comments. Once there are more than 12 to 1 (11.6 to 1 to be exact) positive to negative comments, performance declines, possibly because there is not enough reality checking and constructive feedback occurring (Fredrickson and Losada, 2005).

Conclusion

The demands on organizations, and thus teams, are increasing constantly as a result of globalization, environmental stewardship requirements, and rising expectations from stakeholders to meet higher and higher standards of ethics, transparency, and financial diligence. As a result, we are in what has been referred to as "VUCA" times; that is volatile, uncertain, complex and ambiguous (Johansen, 2007). The High Performance Team Coaching system is a useful approach for leaders and coaches to structure and support teams to move from good to great. The HPTC system helps teams focus on what their purpose is, establish actions to achieve their goals, come together as a stronger and more interdependent team, and continuously learn and adapt throughout their work together.

As you implement the HPTC system, we hope that you have as much success with your teams as we have had with ours. We look forward to hearing about your successes and welcome your questions and comments as you implement the High Performance Team Coaching system.

Feel free to contact us through our websites for more information about the HPTC system or our executive and team coaching services.

www.InnerActiveLeadership.ca
www.CatherineCarr.ca
www.HighPerformanceTeamCoaching.com

Appendix

Appendix 1: Research Behind the High Performance Team Coaching System

TEAM STAGE AND COACHING FUNCTION	TEAM COACHING COMPONENTS	RESEARCH / LITERATURE REVIEW
Central to model (throughout coaching)	Safety	• Team safety is linked to enhanced performance. (Edmondson, 1999) and innovation (Buljac-Samardžic, 2012).
Beginning → Define and Initiate	1. Assessment	• Six conditions for team effectiveness (Wageman, Nunes, Burruss and Hackman, 2008). • Team Diagnostic Survey (Wageman, Hackman and Lehman, 2005).
	2. Coaching for Team Design	• Six conditions for team effectiveness (Wageman et al., 2008). • Team design links to team effectiveness (Beckhard, 1972; Friedlander and Brown, 1974; Hackman and Wageman, 2005; Kaplan, 1979; Wageman, 2001).
	3. Team Launch	• Team offsite included in team coaching (Anderson, Anderson and Mayo, 2008; Blattner and Bacigalupo, 2007; Clutterbuck, 2007; Guttman, 2008; Hackman, 2011; Kegan and Lahey, 2009).

TEAM STAGE AND COACHING FUNCTION	TEAM COACHING COMPONENTS	RESEARCH / LITERATURE REVIEW
	4. Individual Coaching	• Team leader coaching is beneficial (Hawkins, 2011; Wageman et al., 2008). • Individual coaching is included (Anderson, et al., 2008; Blattner and Bacigalupo, 2007; Clutterbuck, 2007; Haug, 2011; Mulec and Roth, 2005; Woodhead, 2011).
Midpoint → Review and Realign	5. Ongoing Team Coaching	• Follow-up sessions are included (Guttman, 2008; Hawkins, 2011). • Structured team coaching session format called GROUP and RE-GROUP (Brown and Grant, 2010).
Ending → Reassess and Integrate	6. Review Learning and Successes	• Reflection and learning facilitated team safety and innovation (Buljac-Samardžic, 2012). • Team reflection and learning is important in coaching (Clutterbuck, 2007; Hackman, 2003; Kegan and Lahey, 2009).
Outcomes	Team Effectiveness	• Three measures of team effectiveness (Wageman et al., 2008).

High Performance Team Coaching

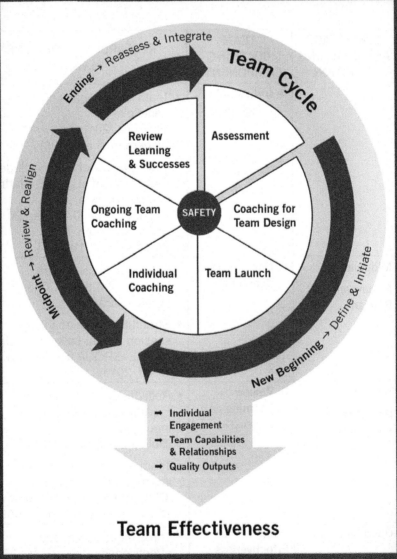

Team Cycle

- Ending → Reassess & Integrate
- Midpoint → Review & Realign
- New Beginning → Define & Initiate

Review Learning & Successes

Assessment

Ongoing Team Coaching

SAFETY

Coaching for Team Design

Individual Coaching

Team Launch

→ Individual Engagement
→ Team Capabilities & Relationships
→ Quality Outputs

Team Effectiveness

High Performance Team Coaching

A comprehensive and systemic approach designed to support a team
to maximize its collective talents and resources
to accomplish and exceed the goals required by the organization.

TEAM CHARTER ON A PAGE TEMPLATE
Team Name - Date

Vision		
Team Mission or Mandate or Purpose		
Team Members	**Working Agreements**	**Key Goals**
Values		**Success Measures**

"**High Performance Team Coaching**
(HPTC) is a fantastic resource and a
'must read' for all Team Leaders and
Coaches. The authors demystify the
concepts of creating and sustaining
high performance teams and how to
lead and coach them… it is a resource
that will help move your team from
average or good, to high performance
in any context."

- Lillas Marie Hatala & Richard Hatala,
Co-authors of *Integrative Leadership*

Also by Peters and Carr

Dr. Jacqueline Peters, PCC, CHRP
is an Executive Coach, author and
Organizational Consultant with
over 20 years of internal and
external experience improving
the business performance of
leaders, teams and organizations.
Dr. Peters is the founder of
InnerActive Leadership Associates.

Dr. Catherine Carr, PCC, RCC
is an Executive Coach, author and
Organizational Consultant with
over 20 years of experience
guiding individuals, teams
and organizations to
realize their fullest potential.
Dr. Carr is the founder of
Catherine Carr and Associates.

Jacqueline.Peters@InnerActive.ca
www.InnerActiveLeadership.ca

Dr.CatherineCarr@gmail.com
www.CatherineCarr.ca

InnerActive

www.HighPerformanceTeamCoaching.com

References and Resources for Further Reading

Anderson, M., Anderson, D., and Mayo, W. (2008) Team coaching helps a leadership team drive cultural change at caterpillar. *Global Business and Organizational Excellence*, 27(4), pp.40-50.

Beckhard, R. (1972) Optimizing team building effort. *Journal of Contemporary Business*, 1(3), pp.23-32.

Blattner, J., and Bacigalupo, A. (2007) Using emotional intelligence to develop executive leadership and team and organisational development. *Consulting Psychology Journal: Practice and Research*, 59(3), pp.209-219.

Brown, S.W., and Grant, A.M. (2010) From GROW to GROUP: theoretical issues and a practical model for group coaching in organisations. *Coaching: An International Journal of Theory, Research and Practice*, 3(1), pp.30-45.

Buljac-Samardžić, M. (2012) *Healthy teams: analyzing and improving team performance in long term care*. Ph.D. thesis, Erasmus University.

Cardon, A. (2003) *Le coaching d'equipes [Team coaching]*. Paris, France: Editions d'Organisation.

Carr, C., and Peters, J. (2012) *The experience and impact of team coaching: a dual case study*. Doctoral dissertation, Middlesex University.

Carr, C., and Peters, J. (2013) The experience and impact of team coaching: a dual case study. *International Coaching Psychology Review*, 8(1), pp.80-98.

Carr, C., and Peters, J. (2013) *The team coaching readiness checklist essentials*. Forthcoming.

Clutterbuck, D. (2007) *Coaching the team at work*. London: Good News Press.

Corporate Leadership Council (2011). *The power of peers: building engagement capital through peer interaction* [Internet]. Available from: http://greatmanager.ucsf.edu/files/CLC_The_Power_of_Peers_Building_Engagement_Capital_Through_Peer_Interaction.pdf [Accessed 31 January 2013]

Cox, E. (2012) Individual and organizational trust in a reciprocal peer coaching context. *Mentoring & Tutoring: Partnership in Learning*, 20(3), pp. 427-443.

Coyne, K., and Coyne, S. (2011) *Brainsteering: a better approach to break-through ideas*. NY: Harper Collins Publishers.

Cross R., Gray. P., Cunningham. S., Showers, M., and Thomas, R.J. (2010) The Collaborative Organization: How to Make Employee Networks Really Work. *MIT Sloan Review* [Internet]
Available from: http://sloanreview.mit.edu/article/the-collaborative-organi-zation-how-to-make-employee-networks-really-work/
[Accessed January, 2013].

Devillard, O. (2005) *La dynamique d'equipes [Team dynamics]*, 3rd edition. Paris, France: Editions d'Organisation.

Edmondson, A. (1999) Psychological safety and learning behavior in work teams. *Administrative Science Quarterly*, 4(2), pp.350-383.

Edmondson, A. (2012) Teaming: *how organizations learn, innovate, and compete in the knowledge economy*. San Francisco, CA: Jossey-Bass.

Fredrickson, B., and Losada, M. (2005) Positive affect and the complex dynamics of human flourishing. *American Psychologist*, 60(7), pp.678-686.

Gersick, C. (1988) Time and transition in work teams: toward a new model of group development. *Academy of Management Journal*, 31(1), pp.9-41.

Gottman, J. (1994) *What predicts divorce: the relationship between marital processes and marital outcomes*. Hillsdale, New Jersey: Lawrence Erlbaum Associates.

Gottman, J. (2011) *The science of trust: emotional attunement for couples*. New York: Norton & Company Inc.

Guttman, H. (2008) *Great business teams: cracking the code for standout performance*. Hoboken, New Jersey: John Wiley and Sons.

Hackman, J.R. (2002) *Leading teams: setting the stage for great performances*. Boston: Harvard Business School Press.

Hackman, J.R. (2003) Learning more by crossing levels: evidence from airplanes, hospitals, and orchestras. *Journal of Organizational Behavior*, 24, pp.905-922.

Hackman, J.R. (2011) Six common misperceptions about teamwork. *Har vard Business Review* [Internet blog]. Available from: http://blogs.hbr.org/cs/2011/06/six_common_misperceptions_abou.html [Accessed 23 June 2011].

Hackman, J.R. (2012) From causes to conditions in group research. *Journal of Organizational Behavior*, 33(3), pp.428–444.

Hackman, J.R., and O'Connor, M. (2005) *What makes for a great analytic team? Individual vs. team approaches to intelligence analysis.* Washington, DC: Intelligence Science Board, Office of the Director of Central Intelligence.

Hackman, J.R., and Wageman, R. (2005) A theory of team coaching, *Academy of Management Review*, 30(2), pp.269–287.

Haug, M. (2011) What is the relationship between coaching interventions and team effectiveness? *International Journal of Evidence Based Coaching and Mentoring*, Special Issue No.5, pp.89-101.

Hawkins, P. (2011) *Leadership team coaching: developing collective transformational leadership.* Philadelphia, PA: Kogan Page Publishers.

Horvath, A., and Symonds, D. (1991) Relation between working alliance and outcome in psychotherapy: a meta-analysis. *Journal of Counseling Psychology*, 38(2), pp.139-149.

Johansen, B. (2007) *Get there early: sensing the future to compete in the present.* San Francisco: Berrett-Koehler Publishers.

Kaplan, R. (1979) The conspicuous absence of evidence that process consultation enhances task performance. *Journal of Applied Behavioral Science*, 15, pp.346-360.

Katzenbach, J., and Smith, D. (1993) *The wisdom of teams: creating the high-performance organization.* Boston: Harvard Business School.

Kegan, R., and Lahey, L. (2009) *Immunity to change.* Boston: Harvard Business Publishing School.

Marshall, M.K. (2006) *The critical factors of coaching practice leading to successful coaching outcomes.* Ph.D. thesis, Antioch University.

Moral, M. (2009) Executive team coaching in mulitnational companies. In M. Moral, and G. Abbott (Eds.), *The Routledge companion to international coaching* (pp. 256-268). London: Routledge.

Moral, M. Vallee, S., and Lamy, F. (2011) Measuring the capability of a team to fulfill a "change 2". In I. O'Donnovan and D. Megginson (Eds.) *Developing mentoring and coaching research practice* (pp. 42-50). Proceedings from the 1st EMCC research conference; University of Twente, Enschede, Netherlands, July 7-8, 2011. Sheffield, U.K.: European Mentoring and Coaching Council.

Mulec, K., and Roth, J. (2005) Action, reflection, and learning and coaching in order to enhance the performance of drug development project management teams. *R and D Management*, 35, pp.483-491.

Parsons, A., and Carr C. (2013) Strategic partnerships and external innovation. Pharma Focus Asia, 18, Forthcoming. [Internet]

Peters, J. (2013) *High performance team coaching assessment.* Forthcoming.

Peters, J. and Carr, C. (2013) *50 tips for terrific teams.* Calgary, Alberta: InnerActive Leadership Associates Inc.

Tuckman, B. (1965) Developmental sequence in small groups. *Psychological Bulletin*, 63(6), pp.384-389.

Wageman, R. (2001) How leaders foster self-managing team effectiveness: design choices versus hands-on coaching. *Organization Science*, 12, pp.559-577.

Wageman, R., Hackman, J.R., and Lehman, E. (2005) Team diagnostic survey: development of an instrument. *Journal of Applied Behavioral Science*, 41, pp.373-398.

Wageman, R., Nunes, D., Burruss, J., and Hackman, J.R. (2008) *Senior leadership teams: what it takes to make them great.* Boston: Harvard Business School Publishing Corporation.

Wageman, R., Fisher, C., and Hackman, J.R. (2009) Leading teams when the timing is right: finding the best moments to act. *Organizational Dynamics*, 38(3), pp.192-203.

Watson Wyatt Work Study (2008) *Driving business results through continuous engagement* (2008/2009 WorkUSA Survey Report). USA, Watson Wyatt Worldwide.

Woodhead, V. (2011) How does coaching help to support team working? A case study in the NHS. *International Journal of Evidence Based Coaching and Mentoring*, Special Issue No.5, pp.102-119.

Woolley, A., Gerbasi, M., Chabris, C., Kosslyn, S., and Hackman, J.R. (2007) Using brain-based measures to compose teams: how individual capabilities and team collaboration strategies jointly shape performance. *Social Neuroscience*, 2(2), pp.96-105.

Woolley, A., Gerbasi, M., Chabris, C., Kosslyn, S., and Hackman, J.R. (2008) Bringing in the experts: how team composition and collaborative planning jointly shape analytic effectiveness. *Small Group Research*, 39, pp.352-371.

About the Authors

Jacqueline Peters, B.Sc., M.Ed., DProf, PCC, CHRP

Executive coach and team and leadership specialist Dr. Jacqueline Peters has over 20 years of experience coaching leaders, executives, and teams to achieve higher performance. Jacqueline's clients say that her unique mix of practical corporate experience and doctoral level knowledge of leadership, coaching, and team effectiveness helps them achieve and exceed their personal and team productivity goals. She and Dr. Catherine Carr co-developed the High Performance Team Coaching System, a robust approach developed for leaders and coaches that is grounded in the research and proven practices that build team effectiveness.

Prior to coaching and facilitating leadership teams through her own company, Jacqueline spent many years working as a senior leader focused on management and leadership development in large corporations. Jacqueline is a professional member of the Canadian Association of Professional Speakers (CAPS), and a professional certified coach (PCC) with the International Coaching Federation (ICF). She has a Doctorate (DProf) in Leadership Development and Coaching from Middlesex University (UK), specializing in team coaching. The dissertation that she co-authored with Catherine Carr was awarded the Ken Goulding award for the most outstanding professional doctorate at Middlesex University in 2012.

Catherine Carr, B.Sc., M.Ed., DProf, PCC, RCC

Catherine has 20 years of experience in leadership development, group and team coaching, coach training and supervision, and program facilitation. She offers evidence-based approaches to coaching and organizational development. Catherine is known for her warmth and confidence building approach. She supports and motivates leaders and teams to imagine their ideal and make it real.

In 2011 Catherine helped design and launch the British Columbia Public Service Agency's innovative team coaching service, which is embarking on team coaching services for potentially 26,000 staff. Her current work includes developing coaching culture initiatives for organizations, of which team coaching is an essential component. Catherine is a professional certified coach (PCC) with the International Coaching Federation (ICF). She has a Doctorate (DProf) in Leadership Development and Executive Coaching from Middlesex University (UK), specializing in team coaching. She co-developed the High Performance Team Coaching system underlying this book with Dr. Jacqueline Peters. The dissertation that she co-authored with Jacqueline Peters was awarded the Ken Goulding Award for the most outstanding professional doctorate at Middlesex University in 2012.

CPSIA information can be obtained
at www.ICGtesting.com
Printed in the USA
LVOW03s0217280917
550349LV00011B/883/P